Help Your
Boys
Succeed

Help Your
Boys
Succeed

The essential guide for parents

Gary Wilson

network
continuum

Continuum International Publishing Group

Network Continuum
The Tower Building   80 Maiden Lane, Suite 704
11 York Road   New York
SE1 7NX   NY 10038

www.networkcontinuum.co.uk
www.continuumbooks.com

Photographs by Phil Richards © Anthony Gell School

Thanks to Will, Andy, Liam and Luke and all the students at Anthony Gell School, Wirksworth, Derbyshire for their cooperation and inspiration.

British Library Cataloguing-in-Publication Data

A catalogue record for this book is available from the British Library.

ISBN: 9-781-855-39449-0 (paperback)

Library of Congress Cataloguing-in-Publication Data
Wilson, Gary B.
Help your boys succeed : the essential guide for parents / Gary Wilson.
        p. cm. -- (Help your child succeed)
ISBN 978-1-85539-449-0
1. Boys. 2. Success in children. 3. Self-esteem in children.
4. Child rearing. 5. Parenting. 6. Parent and child. I. Title. II. Series.

HQ775.W55 2008
649'.132--dc22   2008018931

Typeset by Ben Cracknell Studios
Printed and bound in Great Britain by MPG Books, Cornwall

Contents

Introduction

Girls outperform boys at every subject in GCSE

Boys falling behind in English

Gender gap fails to close

Laddish behaviour blamed for boys' failure

Every year, when examination results come out, the papers are full of the news that boys are falling behind girls in terms of their achievement. Regularly the papers blame the way boys are these days – the so-called 'laddish' culture. Sometimes commentators blame the fact that boys are not doing so well on the lack of female teachers. Similarly they will often cite the lack of male role models in our society generally and the lack of male role models in the family as reasons for the lack of male achievement. At its most extreme, we can even sometimes hear people claiming that it's all down to a worsening of discipline in schools. This gang are normally heard baying for a return to corporal punishment, claiming 'That'll sort the little devils out!' Taken on their own, any one of the above ideas is far too simplistic, missing as they do a wide range of far more subtle causes for boys' underperformance in school.

Of course, there are issues around laddish culture, but there's nothing new there – hieroglyphics from ancient Egypt refer to youths creating antisocial disturbances. More recently, hooligans and groups of young men known as the Scuttlers used to terrorize the streets in Victorian times.

Certainly, it is true that there is a significant lack of male teachers in our schools, particularly in primary schools. The proportion of male teachers under the age of 30 in schools in the UK, both primary and secondary, is currently around 5 per cent. In fact almost half the pupils in primary schools in the UK will not be taught by a male teacher until they reach high school. This is significant, particularly where there is no adult male role model in the home either. However, research suggests overwhelmingly that it is not the gender of teachers that counts but their quality, and the quality of the relationships that teachers are able to develop with their pupils counts the most. Many parents (not you of course!) have been crying out for more male teachers in school 'To DO the discipline and take the football.' WRONG. I know from talking to many, many boys that the kind of male teachers that they like are the ones who they can have a laugh with (and boys are very clear on this point) and the ones who don't let things go too far. In other words, boys like male teachers who are firm but fair, with clear boundaries. Recently I visited a primary school where a group of boys had written poems about their teachers. I copied down some extracts:

- Mr Nash is a chocolate bar, nice and creamy.
- Mr Farrington is a glass of red wine that gets better with age.
- Mr Copnall is a drink of fizzy Coke.
- Mr Malacaso is the month of June when the sun comes out.

If you're male and considering teaching, take note! If we need more male teachers in our schools, then the kind we need are those who show a more caring side of masculinity, particularly if that is what we are trying to develop in our boys, helping to guide them away from those laddish aspects that are preventing them from achieving in school.

There are issues around the lack of positive role models in society at large. We are told that over 70 per cent of youngsters today believe that the way to become rich and successful in life is to become a celebrity in sport, entertainment, reality TV and so on. When we explore their favoured sport stars and entertainers, it can often feel that the negative male role models significantly outweigh the positive. In this sense there is clearly an issue.

The debate has also very much centred around the fact that many boys appear to prefer to learn in ways that are different from the accepted norm in schools. Indeed, as we shall see later, there are issues around what we refer to as preferred learning styles, but again it is more than that.

The fact is that the barriers to boys' achievement are numerous and, to make matters even more confusing, no two boys are alike. If there was a reason why boys underachieve, and therefore just one thing that we needed to do to set the world to rights, then schools would have already done it. The fact is that the problem is complex. This book seeks to explain the complexity of the issue and, most importantly, provide some practical ideas for you as parents to help support your son in fulfilling his potential.

So how much do you know about the scale of the problem?

In England, pupils are first assessed in school at the age of 4–5 in the Foundation Stage, where we measure them in 13 different ways. Over the period of the first three years we have discovered the following to be true:

Foundation Stage Profile

Percentage of pupils who have met or who are working beyond early learning goals in:

Disposition and attitudes	G 64%	B 51%
Social development	G 58%	B 46%
Emotional development	G 61%	B 48%
Language for communication and thinking	G 55%	B 44%
Linking sounds and letters	G 41%	B 31%
Reading	G 43%	B 35%
Writing	G 38%	B 26%
Numbers as labels and for counting	G 60%	B 55%
Calculating	G 44%	B 40%
Shape, space and measure	G 52%	B 47%
Knowledge and understanding of the world	G 52%	B 50%
Physical development	G 68%	B 56%
Creative development	G 58%	B 42%

Some of the largest gaps are, as can be seen, in the four areas to do with language – early reading, writing, language for communication and linking sounds and letters. To understand why this is the case we need to consider the differences in language development between boys and girls. What we know, from considerable amounts of research, is that girls tend to use more language in their early play, between ten and 30 times as much. Consider young girls at play with their friends, and consider the type of play they most frequently indulge in. Creating and acting out stories with their dolls and toys is most common, while boys will tend to be engaged in more active play. In the playground at infant and junior school, boys will often be seen running around being 'Power Rangers', while girls are more likely to be seen standing around in circles 'keeping the oral tradition alive' – playing rhyme games, skipping games, or standing with an adult so that they can have an intelligent conversation. Some of the smaller gaps in the Foundation Stage Profile that favour girls often come as a surprise to parents and teachers alike. What about 'Knowledge and understanding of the world'? Surely boys are knowledge-greedy little creatures? They love dipping into 'Horrible Histories' and 'The Megasuperbookofirrelevantfactoids', and they still quote them in the pub when they're 50! Maybe so, but girls are still marginally in the lead in this area statistically. How about 'Shape, space and measure'? Surely males have at least got superior spatial awareness? Not necessarily so. We can no longer suggest that men are best at reversing cars into parking spaces and that women are best at describing how to do this! Perhaps the biggest surprise to parents among all the results is the difference between boys and girls in terms of physical development. At this point we are measuring a significant amount of gross motor skills – the kind that get those arms throwing that ball and those little legs charging around the playground – and we are also measuring an awful lot of fine motor skills – the kind that get those tiny fingers wrapped efficiently around a pencil and move it across a page in a clearly defined pattern (or not, as the case may be). How many boys (or men for that matter) do you know who have developed a fine, cursive handwriting of which they feel justifiably proud?

And how many boys do you know who have been surrounded by girls throughout their school life who have been told 'That's beautifully neat, dear', and then the teacher (or parent) has just moaned or grimaced at the boys' poor efforts? It is now well understood that the development of fine motor skills in boys is roughly a year behind that of girls by the age of 9. The bottom line is that for a long time we have been forcing many boys to write before they are physically and emotionally ready, and for this reason many have been given an early taste of failure from which they can take a long time to recover. As good parents, we have often been caught up in the same frenzy and panic to ensure that boys are up to scratch with their writing, often panicking if they can't manage at least their name before they start school. Go to him now and tell him the problems with handwriting that have often affected his confidence and self-esteem and slowed him down in tests and exams are not his fault! If you feel you applied too much pressure at the time, don't worry – it's not your fault either. You were doing what we as parents have always done – what we consider to be best for our children. In schools more and more work is now being done to develop those particular skills, using a range of exercises before pen hits paper. We'll explore some later.

What is interesting is that there is one country in the developed world where there is no difference between boys and girls in terms of their achievement – Finland. And what happens there? They don't start school until the age of 7. There are other factors involved too, it has to be said – the fact that Finland is such a literate country where everybody reads and virtually all TV programmes carry subtitles also helps. In another Scandinavian country, Denmark, the 'Forest School' approach is the way in which youngsters experience education; in other words, outdoors, and in a very active way. Such approaches are now beginning to appear in some areas of the UK. The view of some educationalists there is that work on literacy prior to the age of 7 is actually abuse. (We'll look later at ways in which parents can sanely help support early literacy.)

So what happens as boys get older? The first set of tests that schools formally administer are SATs at the end of Key Stage 1 (at the age of 7) in mathematics, science, reading and writing. In these tests girls have outperformed boys nationally since the tests began, particularly in reading and writing. At the age of 11, the same subjects are assessed, and again girls are currently in the lead in all areas, apart from mathematics. So, do things get better as boys get older? What do you think? The bottom line is that many boys believe that they will – in fact some of them think they will without them having to put in any effort! (Do you know anyone like that? If so, try the following quiz with them.)

1

QUIZ

Who does best at Key Stage 3:

Girls or boys? In…ENGLISH?

Girls or boys? In…MATHS?

Girls or boys? In…SCIENCE

Answers

Girls have been doing better in all of these tests, particularly English, since they began in the early 1990s.

1

2

QUIZ

Who do you think does best at GCSE in the following subjects, boys or girls?

Art

Modern Languages

English

Maths

Science

Design Technology

PE

Answers:

Girls have been doing better in all the above subjects for some time now – indeed, girls outperform boys in every single subject at GCSE.

Do things improve at A Level? No. At university? No. Well over half of the entries to university in recent times have been young women, and there are now more young women in management and training colleges.

(If your son has been doing the quiz with you, he might by now be getting mad. That's fine – tell him 'Don't just get mad – get even!')

So what are the reasons? What are schools doing about it? And, most importantly, how can you as parents help improve the situation?

To begin we need to be aware of some extremely important facts:

1   Not all boys are the same!

2   Not all boys are in danger of under-achieving, and for those who are the causes are often quite different.

The main point to remember though is that boys are, without doubt, as capable as girls. Don't tell me boys can't concentrate – have you seen a boy playing a computer game for seven hours non-stop! Don't tell me boys don't have energy or that they never get enthusiastic about things. Don't tell me they are never creative or imaginative. All our boys are perfectly capable of achieving in a variety of ways. So how can we begin to bring these elements to the surface? We need to explore some of the most significant barriers to boys' achievement and consider how we break them down. The following chapters focus on the specific barriers upon which parents, I believe, can have a significant impact. In Chapter 4 I provide a full summary of all the barriers, highlighting the kinds of things that schools are currently working on to raise boys' achievement.

In small discussion groups across the length and breadth of the country, boys have freely offered their insights into why some boys are not doing as well as most girls. They are the real experts and they also know what it is they need to do to put the situation right. I have liberally sprinkled this book with their thoughts on the matter. Every single comment has been repeated to me in various forms, over a number of years. Perhaps you might like to use their comments to stimulate debate in your household.

Chapter 1

The barriers to boys' achievement and how parents can help boys to break through them

Barrier 1: Too much pressure pre-school

We have seen how it can be a significant issue for some boys progressing through school still nursing a sense of failure because they might not be physically or emotionally ready for the taxing demands of learning. As parents, however, we always want to ensure that we are doing the very best for our boys, making sure that they have the best start. There is a fine line between providing support and applying too much pressure. The chart below might start you thinking about how you could take your foot off the pedal in one sense, but drive purposefully onwards in the right direction in another, enabling you to deliver your son at the door, excited not overwhelmed, eager but not anxious, confident not concerned. All this could, and indeed should, be learned through play.

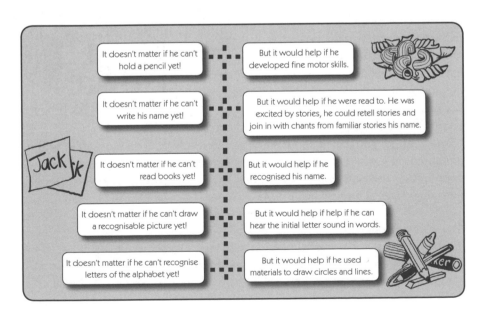

It doesn't matter if he can't hold a pencil yet!

But it would help if he developed fine motor skills.

It doesn't matter if he can't write his name yet!

But it would help if he were read to. He was excited by stories, he could retell stories and join in with chants from familiar stories his name.

Jack

It doesn't matter if he can't read books yet!

But it would help if he recognised his name.

It doesn't matter if he can't draw a recognisable picture yet!

But it would help if help if he can hear the initial letter sound in words.

It doesn't matter if he can't recognise letters of the alphabet yet!

But it would help if he used materials to draw circles and lines.

Fine motor skills can be developed using screw-topped lids, sorting pasta or dried beans, using tweezers, scrunching up newspaper, popping bubble wrap and so on.

Sticky labels with his name and other names around the house can be a fun way of developing word recognition, while a vast and exciting array of writing materials will provide lots of opportunity to make marks. As boys get a little older, toys such as 'Magnadoodles' and 'Aquamats', which allow free drawing and writing that can be made to disappear instantly, can be massively engaging. Writing implements featuring their favourite superheroes or cartoon characters can also encourage writing and drawing in a subtle way. There are countless ways of developing not only language skills but also numeracy through play and a creative approach to day-to-day life with your toddler, such as sorting and matching shells, pasta shapes, beads, jars, clothes, going shopping, making models. But the big word here is play – play not pressure.

Barrier 2: Lack of independence

By and large, teachers will tell you that girls tend to be far more independent when starting school. I have heard countless tales of boys standing around at the beginning of their first few days in nursery or reception, both arms held aloft, waiting to have their jumpers taken off and, at the end of the day, both arms akimbo, waiting to have their coats put on.

Often I will hear of boys, after their PE session in the infants school, sitting on those little benches underneath the little hooks with the little pictures of the little tractors next to them, while the girls are helping them to get dressed, doing up their shirt buttons and fastening their shoelaces. I hear countless tales of boys being asked to tidy up in primary school and they just put anything anywhere or give it to a girl. Pretty embarrassing if you're the parent of a boy isn't it? Yet it would appear from my countless experiences of parents' evenings that some parents are still packing their sons' bags at the age of 14 or 15.

One headteacher recently told me of a conversation he had with a mother who arrived in school to meet with him, clearly perplexed at her son's inability to deliver his GCSE coursework: 'I just can't understand it Mr Robinson, why Michael isn't doing the work for you, you know, because he has every opportunity to do it. I do everything for him at home you know, Mr Robinson.' Then she continued, proudly, 'I take him his breakfast in bed every day.' Adding, in a homely and almost conspiratorial fashion, 'Of course you know, I don't butter his toast downstairs, as it makes the toast all soggy. I always take the butter up on a separate plate.' There was a pause, she lost in a reverie, he in incredulity. 'Indeed, Mr Robinson, I've no idea why he doesn't do the work for you.' Of the two of them in the room, she was the only one who didn't appear to know the answer to that question. An extreme example, of course, and clearly there was no intention here other than to do the very best for the boy. But the outcome? Surely, it must almost go without saying that, if we do everything for our boys then we disadvantage them in so many ways, not least in their ability to become independent and successful learners.

One primary headteacher told me recently that she delivered a questionnaire to a group of 8 and 9 year olds and one of the questions was 'Who is responsible for your learning?' Every single girl answered, 'Me. I'm responsible for my learning.' Guess how many boys put that they were? None. Not a single one. They all put 'my teacher', 'my headteacher' or 'my parents'.

It is well understood in education that there is a significant correlation between being independent and being an effective learner. What is more, self-esteem develops as a result of becoming capable of doing things for ourselves. So how can we develop our boys as more independent learners, and subsequently also raise their self-esteem right from the start and all the way through their learning processes? If we don't, we will continue to recreate the cycle described below.

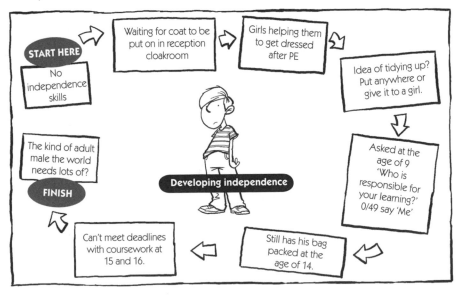

To begin with we need to:

- Make sure he has a list of things he needs for school that day – don't pack his bag for him.
- Encourage him to take decisions on matters that will directly affect him.
- Encourage him to take responsibility for specific jobs around the house that are appropriate to his age.
- Guide him towards a good use of pocket money, but let him make decisions too.
- Let him do things his way sometimes – not always the way you want them!
- Encourage time spent alone without TV or computer.
- Teach him basic time management – 'During the next few days you've got this, this and this to fit in. When are you going to find time for this, this and this?' (You may even be able to relate it to time management in your own sphere of work.)
- When asking him to keep his bedroom tidy, be specific! Chunk the information. 'Tidy your room!' is too vague; try 'Put all your dirty clothes in the basket', 'Put all your CDs in the rack', 'Hang all your clean clothes in the wardrobe', 'Make your bed' and so on.
- Explain to him that for many, many adults, real happiness comes from being independent, and the more independent they are the happier they become.

- In early adolescence, explain that preparation for independent living should be the motivator. Being able to operate all household appliances should be a source of pride – even rites of passage!

Try out some of the following useful phrases:

Barrier 3: Boys starting school linguistically less developed

The fact that less than half the homes in the UK have tables around which families sit and eat and talk on a regular basis clearly has an impact on early language development. It is worth noting that in countries such as Spain, France and Italy, issues surrounding the development of language are far less common. The fact that our homes now are largely centrally heated means that families no longer need to congregate in the same room. Experts point to other issues too, such as the fact that most pushchairs now face away from the parent, so reducing opportunities for verbal interaction. They also tell us that currently 40 per cent of 4 year olds now have televisions in their own bedrooms. One expert suggests:

> It is quite possible that parents are talking to their children less now than at any time during the history of mankind.

Bearing in mind, as previously noted, that girls use between ten and 30 times as much language in their play, the implications for boys are particularly serious.

So how can you help? The simple answer is: Talk! Talk! Talk! But how do we create opportunities for talk with our youngest and how do we get them to engage in conversation as they get older? Here are a few ideas.

Talk! Talk! Talk!

When he's younger:

- Don't put him under pressure to name things but if he does, give him lots of praise.

- Older females and males need to read to him extensively and talk about the reading (and don't stop when he starts to be able to read for himself!).

- Play imaginatively together, talk about what you are doing as you are doing it and encourage him to do the same. Develop characters' voices as you play and encourage him to do the same. The more excited and 'into it' you are, the chattier and more engaged he'll become.

- Talk about what you are doing as you carry out everyday activities.

- Enjoy lots of rhymes and songs together.

- Point out all the things you see around you.

- Look at him as you are talking – it shows him that you value him.

- If he says something incorrectly, don't correct it – just say it back to him the correct way.

- Use sing-song or funny voices for characters when you read.

- Point to pictures and use props such as character-related toys or wizards' hats.

- Make up stories together. You can start by telling stories that are familiar to both of you, then add a new twist (such as bringing yourself into the story), then invent a new story using the same basic structure.

- If his grandad lives far away, get him make a CD of stories.

When he's older:

- Play board-games together.

- Find opportunities for discussion related to films or programmes watched together on television.

- Limit leisure time spent passively in front of screens.

- Eat together as regularly as you can, creating a habit of sharing thoughts and feelings about the day as you do it.

- Wash up together. (I know one famous author who improved his relationship with his son by getting rid of the dishwasher!)

- Talk as you do jobs around the house together (sometimes this is the best time for him to talk about his concerns and problems).

- His 'payment' for a ride in mum or dad's taxi can be a proper heart-to-heart.

In general:

- Never stop responding to his questions, or he may just stop asking them.

Was that the Grunt Affirmative, the Grunt Negative or the Grunt Non-committal?

A few years ago the papers were talking about the 'Grunt Culture' being among us. They were referring to the fact that in some poor areas of the UK, white working-class boys were starting school unable to put a sentence together. They might equally have been talking about the occasional adolescent boy whose responses to questions sometimes fall into the 'grunt' category. Questions such as 'Did you have a good day at school?' 'Hrmph!' Questions that may just get him to talk are the kind that can't be answered using one word, be it 'Yes', 'No' or 'Hrmph' (open questions instead of closed ones):

- What was the best question you asked today? (Einstein's parents used to ask him that – it didn't do him any harm.)
- What was the best/funniest/worst/strangest/most exciting thing that happened to you today?

- What are you looking forward to tomorrow?
- Was there anything you didn't understand at school?

If the answer is still limited, and you know that important information is deliberately being blocked, you can ask further questions to release that blockage by following two simple rules. You (a) respond using the language they used with you and (b) ask them to be more specific. Using their language back to them shows respect for their initial statement and their response will flow more as they release the blocks they had initially presented. For example:

'How was your day?'
'It was rubbish. I hate English.'

Now we could say, 'What do you mean by that? Don't be silly, of course you don't hate English!'

We could, but that's likely to be the end of the conversation, because nothing we have said has related to their internal computer which is continuing to tell them that actually yes, at this moment in time, they do hate English because of something that happened today which they would do better articulating. So instead it might go:

'How was your day?'
'It was rubbish, I hate English.'
'What was rubbish?'
'English.' (Still blocking – try again)
'English isn't always rubbish, is it? What was it that made you hate English today?'
'No, it's usually OK really, but today it was just copying stuff out.'
'And you hate just copying stuff out, don't you? But it's usually OK, yes? So what's going OK with the English at the moment?'
'Well, the play we're doing is OK.'

And you're off!

As far as getting him to talk is concerned, you will really hit the jackpot if you get him to teach you something that he has been taught that day – because that is *the* way we learn most effectively. In which case you might care to try:

- Sheep-farming in Australia – I've always wanted to know about that.'
- 'Algebra – wish I could understand that, I always found it difficult.'
- 'What is *Macbeth* all about?'

- (You'll no doubt be able to think of questions that sound more realistic and less patronizing in real life!)
- When you get him in full flow, the bottom line is you're going to have to listen! And learn!

Barrier 4: Physiological needs not met

Are you tired of telling him to get to bed otherwise he will be too tired for school the next day? Tired of constantly having to say to him 'Breakfast is the most important meal of the day?' and yet he steadfastly refuses to eat it.

I know how you feel! I have asked countless groups of 15- and 16-year-old boys in assemblies right across the country how many of them hadn't bothered having breakfast that morning. It is usually about 70 per cent. This seems to be very much a boy-thing as they get older. You might like to share with him the following fact, as I do with other boys: 'If you don't eat breakfast, then by 10.30 your brain will have the reaction speed of a 70-year-olds.' You might like to share the following too, from the experts:

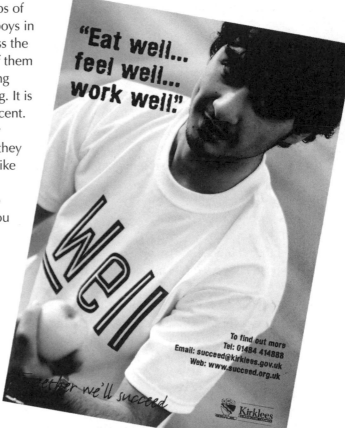

"Eat well... feel well... work well"

To find out more
Tel: 01484 414888
Email: succeed@kirklees.gov.uk
Web: www.succeed.org.uk

Kirklees

- Brains need some sleep! At least eight hours.
- Make sure that you have breakfast cereal, particularly the kind that contains grains as they slowly release energy.
- Think about what you have for lunch and try to make it a healthy option, not too heavy on fat.

- Make sure your brain has fuel! Drink water every day. Space your drinking out over the day so that you never get to the point when you are feeling thirsty. You won't work well if your brain dries up!
- Avoid fizzy drinks. Most fizzy drinks have loads of sugar and other things in them that won't help your brain to work at its best.
- Snacks are great: they can keep your energy level up, but you need to think about what you snack on. Sweets, for example, are mostly full of sugar and fat. To fill that gap and to feed your brain, you need to look for things that are more healthy. Bananas are great brain food.

Of course, in the old days children would line up for their daily dose of cod liver oil, and that was the school's contribution to healthy eating. At the time of writing, virtually every school in the land is now, quite rightly, very involved with healthy eating. There is no room for complacency though – after all, children eat only around 20 per cent of their food in school during the course of a year. As we know, the challenge is to ensure they get the message for the remaining 80 per cent! (Incidentally, also at the time of writing, at least one local authority is supplying all children with omega 3 capsules in the light of persuasive evidence that omega 3 (and 6 and 9) can help keep the brain alert. These elements are more powerful in their raw form in food, but our food is now so tainted with additives that it is extremely difficult for our bodies to extract them.

With regard to physiological needs, they are, as can be seen from the work of Abraham Maslow, the first step towards anyone achieving what they want, need or deserve to achieve in life.

SELF ACTUAL-IZATION

ESTEEM NEEDS

SAFETY NEEDS

PHYSIOLOGICAL NEEDS

Maslow, A. (1954) *Motivation and Personality* (New York: Harper)

Maslow's model simply highlights the fact that before even the basic human need for safety and self-esteem and the need to 'self-actualize' – in other words, to feel like a worthwhile, confident human being – basic physiological needs must be met. He suggests that unless these three sets of needs are fulfilled, then the chances of anyone achieving their potential is unlikely.

Barrier 5: Negative attitudes to writing

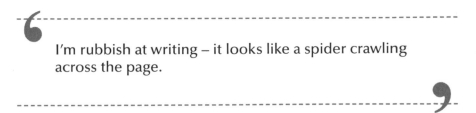

I'm rubbish at writing – it looks like a spider crawling across the page.

As we saw earlier, being forced to write before your fine motor skills are developed can have a significant negative impact in so many ways. So many boys say to me 'writing hurts', and so many don't like writing just because they are frustrated or embarrassed by the way it looks. Exercises to improve handwriting come into fashion and then disappear again. Many of us have painful memories of producing page after page of pretty patterns in the vain hope that our handwriting would also begin to look beautifully symmetrical. Whether a boy is humiliated or depressed about his handwriting or not, the likelihood of getting him to emulate these exercises day after day as he gets older is slim indeed. The following may help (*but too much pressure won't!*):

When he is young:

- Holding a pen correctly might be a problem, so ask him to try this: 'Lay the pen down, point towards you, hold the tip of the pen between first finger and thumb, then flip it over until the pen rests on the fleshy part of the hand between the base of the thumb and first finger.'

- If he writes with the pen facing bolt upright to the sky, try the 'scrunchy' (hair-band) method: wrap a scrunchy around his wrist (just until he gets into the new habit, of course – not for the rest of his life!), expanding it so that it firmly holds down the top of the pen to rest it between the base of the thumb and first finger.

When he is older:

- A national handwriting expert shared the following tip with me. Say to the child, 'Make sure all the sticky-up bits are the same height and that all the rounded bits are the same shape – and practise this for five minutes a day before you do homework.'

At any age:

- Tell him to take a piece of scrap-paper and scrunch it up as tightly as he can in his writing hand, then unfold it again as smoothly as possible, without using the other hand or resting it on anything (a simple warm-up technique – the equivalent of having a kick-about before a game of football, shall we say).

- Give praise, praise and more praise for content (which is, after all, the most important thing) and praise too for any improvement in the presentation of his work.

Why the fuss? The answer is that some boys' self-esteem can suffer because of their handwriting. It is also true that people who struggle with handwriting have to slow down to make themselves clear in exams and, as a result, often don't finish the questions.

Weak spelling can also cause a lack of confidence. Some boys become anxious that their poor spelling will make them fail their exams. Not so, as a very limited number of marks in tests and exams are lost because of it. (A maximum of 5 per cent for handwriting and spelling combined, even in English GCSE.) What is undeniable, however, is the impact on self-esteem. While constant testing at home or at school has limited value, some strategies have 'boy appeal', such as those listed below. But too much pressure causes anxiety and becomes counterproductive.

- Find words in words (in–fir–mary) (sep–a–rate)
- Highlight tricky bits
- Use rhyme
- Segment into syllables
- Exaggerate pronunciation
- Pronounce silent letters
- Chant the letters
- Look, cover, write, say and check (look at a word, cover it, try spelling it, say it out loud, check it's correct, repeat if not).

Again, what is important is to be full of praise for success and not overcritical. Good dictionaries, word-games and computer spellchecks all help.

More worrying than technical problems with handwriting or spelling is a totally negative attitude to writing itself that is all too evident among many boys for a variety of reasons. Some boys have a downer on the amount of writing they have to do because it's physically demanding, or because it takes up too much time – time they'd rather spend discussing ideas or doing something more practical.

> I like lessons where you just talk and you don't have to write it down.

Sometimes boys question the value of what they've been asked to do. They do tend to be the best barometers of good teaching. They can detect a worthless task, such as mindless copying, at a hundred paces.

> It's just boring – copying it from a textbook. Why write it out again?

One 11 year old said the following to me:

> It's a waste of trees, Sir. When you're copying, you don't even read it. You just copy down the patterns the words make on the page.

Many boys initially flounder for ideas when asked to write. However, in schools where they make a lot of use of discussions and role-play, debates, group work and so on, boys find it easier to write. It is now well understood that most boys need the time to think and discuss before they put pen to paper. If he's struggling with a piece of writing at home, one of the best ways to help him is to have a conversation about it with him first – many boys need to talk through their ideas before they can transfer ideas to paper. If it's a piece of discursive writing (putting an argument together) or persuasive writing, have a good discussion with him first.

When I talk to boys of primary age, it always amazes me just how many of them enjoy writing at home – for pleasure! It's usually about the sabre-toothed chicken they've just invented or a new series of *Doctor Who* with them in the starring role. If you discover that he is doing something like this, then praise it to the hilt, value it! But you might think twice before proudly carrying it to his teacher to show it off – this is his space, his playtime.

How parents can support boys' writing

- Encourage wide and varied reading (emphasis on fiction).

- Talk through his ideas with him before he starts to write.

- Encourage him to tackle his writing in 'chunks'.

- Help him to experiment with mapping out ideas using maps, flowcharts, diagrams and so on (see planning and prep).

- Give lots of praise and encouragement and encourage him to take pride in his writing.

- If he's short of ideas, start from what interests him and discuss it, sharing his enthusiasm.

- Try hot-seating a character in a story he's writing or a book he's reading (he has to pretend he is a character in the book and you ask him questions about what he is going through as the character).

- Make sure he feels that he has your genuine interest.

- Reward him regularly.

- Get him to talk about personal experiences before he writes them.

- Get him to describe friends and family as starting-points for developing characters.

- If he has to write a book review, talk to him about the book first and make bullet-points or produce a map.

Barrier 6: Limited interest in reading

There are only two lasting bequests we can hope to give our children. One of these is roots; the other, wings
Hodding Carter

One of the most precious gifts we can give our children is a love of reading. When it comes to our sons the gift is especially powerful. Reading helps us in so many ways. The fact that reading helps us to increase our vocabulary, improve our spelling, improve our punctuation and our understanding of difficult ideas represents only the surface of what reading can do for us. It also awakens our imagination, allows us to explore feelings and relationships and understand important issues on a personal and worldwide level. The fact that recent studies show that 70 per cent of boys in high schools say they don't read is clearly a matter for concern. Even in primary schools we see some boys shying away from reading fiction because they see it as more of a girly thing to do. Boys need to read to succeed for all the reasons above and many more.

Yes, reading will help them with their own writing. Yes, it will help them come to terms with the world. Yes, it will spark ideas for them, but most of all it will slow them down and help them to become more reflective. For this most significant reason of all, boys particularly need to read fiction. Here we sometimes have a problem. A lot of boys only ever see older males reading newspapers or instruction manuals. Some boys may have only been read to by mum and seen only females reading fiction. Some start to believe that reading is this special, magical, mystical thing that girls, mums and female teachers know all about, and they don't want to get involved because they don't want to end up looking silly in front of the opposite (or their own) sex.

Some boys choose to flick through non-fiction books because it hides the fact that they are not confident readers and it's a more boyish thing to do.

Put simply, boys would learn better and do better in school generally if only we could get them to slow down and reflect on their learning. Flicking fairly aimlessly through a 'Bumpergiantmegabookofstuff' isn't going to do the trick – reading fiction will help them develop the vital skill of reflection that so many desperately lack.

When they are younger:

- Books need to be around from the word go!

- Make reading time a very regular, special, fun-filled time for all of you – bring characters to life with actions and voices.

- Have a wide variety of books prominently and attractively displayed in the house.

- Make visiting the library and bookshops a regular part of his weekly routine.

- Make your own books together, using holiday photographs to retell incidents.

- Discuss the stories before (based on the cover) – during (predicting what's going to happen) and afterwards (reviewing the story).

- Make sure, wherever possible, that he is read to by older females *and* older males.

- Don't stop reading to him just because he can read!

As they get older:

- Seeing older males in the house reading and talking about their reading can really help.

- Give books as presents or rewards.

- Encourage him to join a web-based book club.

- Encourage him to explore author websites.

- Take an interest in what he's reading – maybe even read the same book from time to time and discuss it together.

- Find fiction that will relate to their particular interests (see below).

- Books that are TV or film 'tie-ins' can often entice reluctant readers on board.

If he appears to be only interested in one particular series of books on, say, a particular boy wizard – point out to him there are other books in a series/ books about wizards/books about schoolboy heroes/books about imaginary lands – any good bookseller will be able to guide him.

The top end of primary school and the lower end of high school can be a critical time for boys and their reading, but there are so many exciting books out there for boys of that age. Experience suggests that there are key categories of books that particularly appeal. Here are some of them, with particular recommendations.

Boys like books that are in a series:
Artemis Fowl, Young Bond, Captain Underpants, His Dark Materials, Series of Unfortunate Events, Mortal Engines, Edge Chronicles, Windsinger, The Chronicles of Narnia, The Lord of the Rings.

Boys like books that have an edge to them:
Weirdo's War, Creeper, Jake's Tower, Martyn Pig, The Crew, Boy Kills Man, and works by authors such as Benjamin Zephaniah, Anthony Horowitz, Malorie Blackman and Bali Rai.

Boys like books that are about powerful ideas:
Bloodtide, Millions, I am the Cheese, Warriors of the Raven, Wheel of Fire, Feather Boy and works by authors such as Keith Gray, David Almond and Philip Pullman.

Boys like books that draw on myth, legend and fantasy:
The Wizard of Earthsea, Keys to the Kingdom, Beowulf, the Arthurian Legends and Norse sagas, and works by authors such as Alan Garner, Susan Cooper, D. Wynne Jones, Christopher Paolini and Peter Dickinson.

Boys like books that appeal to their sense of mischief:
The Legend of Spud Murphy, Horrid Henry, Jiggy McQue and books by writers such as Roald Dahl, Terry Pratchett, Roddy Doyle, Maurice Gleitzman, Jeremy Strong, Ian Ogilvy, Philip Ridley and Louis Sachar.

Boys like books that are funny:
The Discworld series, Jiggy Stories, Adrian Mole, Little Wolf Stories, Joey Pigza stories, Justin, Just William, Jennings and books by writers such as Douglas Adams, Philip Ardagh, Paul Jennings and Pete Johnson.

> **Boys like books that are plot driven:**
> *Harry Potter*, *Holes*, *Eagle of the Ninth*, *Stravaganza*, *Hatchet*, *Abhorsen*, *Sharpe*, and books by writers such as Theresa Breslin, Cornelia Funke, Charlie Higson, Conn Iggulden, Robert Swindells, Graham Joyce, Jonathan Stroud, Caroline Lawrence, Robert Muchamore, Keith Oppel, Chris Ryan, Darren Shan.

Barrier 7: Inability to plan and prepare effectively

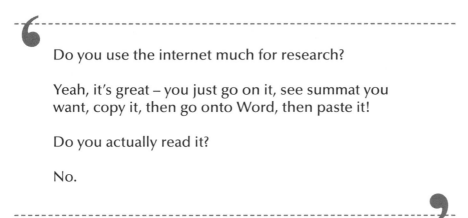

Do you use the internet much for research?

Yeah, it's great – you just go on it, see summat you want, copy it, then go onto Word, then paste it!

Do you actually read it?

No.

For quite a lot of boys, eager to get on with a practical task in, for example, design technology, time spent researching and planning feels like time wasted. Shortcuts seem to be the order of the day, much to their teachers' dismay and to their own detriment. Preparation is all. As one parent suggested to me 'Planning and preparation prevent poor performance!' We aren't born with fully-fledged research skills, and for some people the internet is almost a return to the learned helplessness that once upon a time allowed us to sit back and have our shoelaces fastened at the age of 10. For others, being asked to do internet research is actually quite frightening, like being asked to stare into a great black hole in space. I heard tell of one boy who said to his teacher, 'We don't need you now sir, we've got Google!' Having the internet and knowing how to use it, however, are two completely different things.

When you know he is going to start getting homework, gently offer to do some research with him on the internet. You might research a shared hobby together, or family history or even an outing. Guide him systematically (most boys respond positively to a systematic approach):

1 Ask him to show you what he knows first and how he might approach it. (Many, if not all, of the following steps might not be necessary!)

2 Show him how you make a selection of the most useful search engines.

3 Show him how you make a selection of the most useful websites.

4 Cut and paste chunks that might be useful onto a new word document.

5 Highlight the elements that you definitely want to use, using the highlighter tool.

6 Now, together, put the information you've selected in your own words.

7 Illustrate with pictures collected and selected from a Google image search.

8 Consider appropriate printing formats (e.g. A4 booklet).

Encourage the effective use of computers in other ways too. The assumptions that are often made are that boys and computers are simply made for each other and that plonking a boy in front of a computer will miraculously raise his achievement. Boys love computers mostly because they love playing games on them. They can appear extremely competent on them – that's because they're very competent at playing games on them. A computer will not automatically raise a boy's achievement – it's how he is shown, helped or encouraged to use it that counts. All too often, boys will say to me:

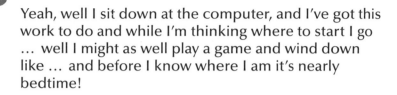

> Yeah, well I sit down at the computer, and I've got this work to do and while I'm thinking where to start I go … well I might as well play a game and wind down like … and before I know where I am it's nearly bedtime!

Yes, computers really can help boys in all sorts of ways, but your encouragement (and occasional monitoring) may be needed. For example, you might:

- Encourage creative presentation – a stock of coloured paper, card, binders and so on can often spice up a project.
- Encourage the effective use of search engines, Frequently Asked Questions, online support and emailing experts in the field.
- Give lots of praise for original and creative work.
- Encourage him to help the younger ones in the family (and you to) use the computer efficiently.
- Encourage him to keep an electronic journal.
- Set him an internet quest as a challenge.

So how else can we help him prepare and plan work?

Brainstorming ideas together on a spider diagram or memory map can really help him to see the big picture before he starts to produce a piece of work. I do feel very strongly that mapping is one of the best strategies around for helping raise boys' achievement. Most boys, after the age of 7, tend to become more left-hemisphere dominant in their brains – and the left hemisphere very much needs to see the big picture. (Interestingly, in a series of 'Dads and Lads' writing projects in primary schools, I introduced mapping for planning stories, and a number of dads and male carers became so taken with the idea they started using mapping at work!)

Creating a memory map

Place the main idea or title, in capitals and in colour, in the centre of a page. Illustrate it. Main ideas then need to be on separate branches, again in capitals. Illustrations need to be added freely (to help plant the ideas visually and aid recall). In the case of a story plan you may include the Who? What? Where? Why? and How?

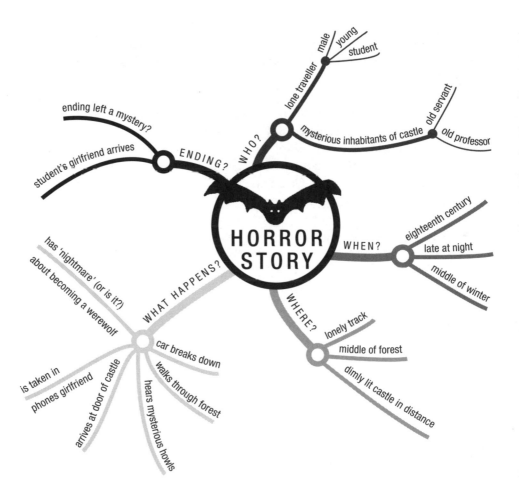

Other tools that can help him with planning and preparation include graphic organizers, so called because they use graphs, diagrams and so on that can help in seeing the big picture. They also provide a system that will allow him to get ideas together in an organized and effective way. Some are very simple, such as the Venn diagram.

Venn diagram

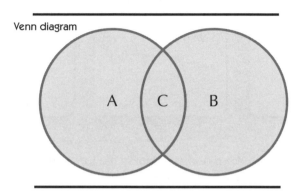

This is useful if he has to make a comparison between things, such as two poems being studied. Important points from one can be entered in A, important points from the other can be entered in B and anything the two poems have in common can be entered in C.

A common thinking-skill tool is called ranking, and is particularly suited to most boys' preferred learning style. Taking the nine most important ideas about something he has to write about and writing each on a small cards (or in text boxes on the computer), he then organizes the cards as follows:

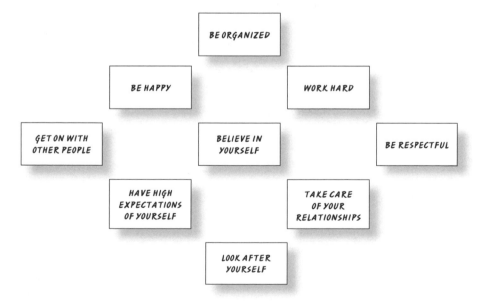

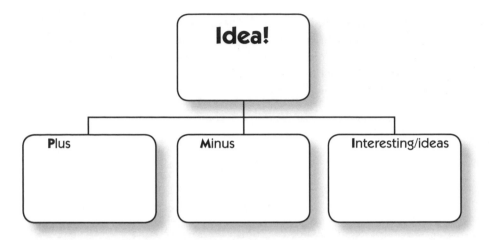

Ideas are arranged with the most important at the top, and then working downwards. (You can have a very interesting discussion with him around the order in which *you* might have placed things.)

Another simple tool to help him get ideas organized is the PMI. Here he writes down the idea and then lists all the pluses, minuses and the interesting things and new ideas that have sprung up. This is useful for putting together balanced arguments and so on.

More complex flow-charts can of course deal with more complex ideas and, again, tend to have quite a lot of boy-appeal due to their systematic nature. Let's say there is a decision to make about a family holiday (trying out this system with 'fun stuff' might just sell the system to him).

1 Ask the family what are all the things they feel are important for a great holiday.
2 Write down the steps you need to follow to achieve your target (these will be represented in rectangular boxes, linked together to show how you move from one step to the next).
3 If there are things you need to make choices about (usually yes or no), these will be put in diamond-shaped boxes.
4 Now draw up the flow-chart!

(The Word programme includes flow-charts under the 'Auto shapes' option.) You might find this a useful approach to help with selecting options in Year 9, or even when thinking about college applications or entering the world of work. It would generate a lot of discussion if you did this together.

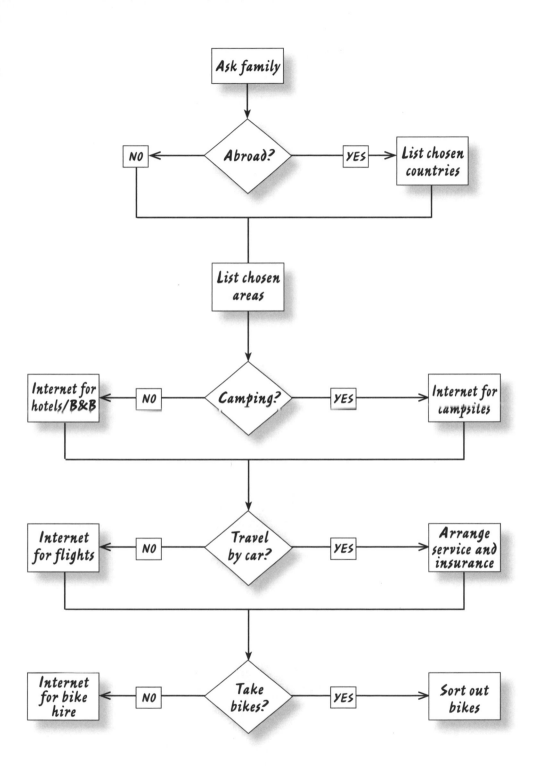

Barrier 8: Peer pressure

'Spodders' in Wiltshire, 'Keeners' in Bristol, 'Squares' in Derbyshire, 'Swots' in Yorkshire and 'Sooks' (because they 'sook' up to their teachers) in Aberdeen are just some of the words schoolchildren use to describe people who work hard across the UK. While some girls suffer from peer pressure, it does seem to be largely a male epidemic. In some primary schools I can occasionally ask the question, 'What do we call people who work hard around here?' and still get responses such as 'Superstar', 'Whizzkid' or 'Brainbox', but those schools are quite rare and seem to becoming rarer still. I call the perpetrators of peer pressure the 'peer police'. I attempt to arm those who want to work hard against the peer police and to encourage the peer police themselves to call off their campaign.

It can start quite early in a boy's school career. One reception teacher told me that she had a routine in her class whereby once someone understood a particular teaching point, as they were all gathered together on the mat, they could leave the mat and get on with their next task. She noticed after a few days of this routine that whenever one particular boy left the mat *all* the other boys left too. She had to quietly ask the little peer police cadet to hold back even though he had understood. The others did too. You hear stories too of peer police cadet controlling playground space and, very frequently, of boys who start primary school wanting to please their teachers but who end up just wanting to please their mates. By the time they get into Years 9 and 10 in some high schools, they are practically running the place as far as providing the unwritten laws for boys is concerned. To younger boys I say, 'When someone is pointing the finger at you, saying "you're a swot, you!", they're pointing three fingers back at themselves saying "I'm stupid, me!"'

I'll sometimes share this poem with them:

You keep calling me swot

You call me prof

You keep calling me crawler

You call me boff

You keep calling me saddo

You call me geek

You keep calling me brainbox

You call me creep

One thing's clear, you're not so bright

YOU … can't even get my name right

But it's not that simple to laugh off something that sometimes strikes right to the heart of a boy's motivation and attitude to learning.

It's a tough call, turning up for the first day at the high school with a violin-case if you're a boy. Peer pressure is a powerful thing in so many ways; it is even responsible for what subjects or what careers boys might follow.

A teacher recently told me that when she was at high school her twin brother was a keen cello player. Every week when they approached school he asked her 'Can you take me cello up to t'music room, sis?' And every week for five years she did. He now plays the cello in a professional orchestra. Thank goodness he had a sister! But it shouldn't have had to be that way.

Together we have to do our best to expose *peer pressure* for what it is – a particularly harmful form of bullying. Why? Because it is something that is the easiest thing in the world to give in to. Who doesn't want to feel part of a gang, group or tribe? Who wants to be isolated, alone or rejected? It is about resilience and strength of character. We have to show boys that as long as they are dancing to someone else's tune, they are never going to be true to themselves. We have to point out that a boy who is going along with the crowd is currently shooting himself in the foot. Remind him that girls are out in front while some boys are currently being their own worst enemies, and say again – 'Don't just get mad, get even!'

> Discuss those boys in school who are calling the tune. Get him to reflect on what it is they are actually doing to themselves – to others – and finally to focus on what they're doing to him. Does it feel good *now* to be listening to the peer police (beware, the answer may well be yes!). How will it feel to be listening to them *just before his exams?* How about *on results day?* How about *ten years from now* when those boys won't even be around?

Many boys suffer peer pressure to some extent. When I am taking an assembly of a whole year-group of boys, it is not unusual for almost half of them to hold up their hands (I ask the whole assembly to close their eyes first) and admit they have been at some time in their school lives bullied or teased because they have worked hard. Ask your son.

> Tell-tale signs of peer pressure:
>
> ● A sudden decision not to take a bag to school.
>
> ● A sudden dip in performance: your high-achieving boy suddenly starts to behave like a low-achiever (he's actively seeking to be 'one of the lads').
>
> ● A pocketful of school merits or credits (he hasn't wanted to hand them in for fear of humiliation).
>
> ● A sudden lack of interest in wanting to celebrate success.
>
> ● A loss of engagement with the arts (subjects perceived by some of the peer police as 'girly').

- A sudden reticence to participate in revision classes, study-support sessions.

To parents of boys of all ages I would say that peer pressure is probably one of the most significant barriers to boys' achievement, and the minute you suspect that you son is under pressure from others not to work, your support and guidance are of paramount importance. If you believe that he is suffering in the same way, you might share the above information with him and also point out that in conversation with hundreds of underachieving 15- and 16-year-old boys over recent years, I often ask how they might have done things differently during their time at school.

> You get faced with a choice – fit in with the lads or get on with your work! And when you have to make that choice early on, the obvious one is to fit in, 'cos when you're young you wanna fit, when you first start high school you don't wanna be picked on … But when you get older, you know, it's too late, you wish you'd done well. My advice? Sometimes you've just got to think about yourself and not about how your mates think about you.   *Carl, 16*

Boys often tell me, 'I would have been a boff', or 'I would have been a swot' – the sense of regret is often very moving.

> I wish I could go back to Year 7. I would have thought about myself instead of everyone else. I wouldn't have messed about at all. I wouldn't have shown off as much, I would have knuckled down – I'd have been a boff. I could've been one, but I turned it down, I wanted to be one of the lads.   *Simon, 16*

You also need discreetly to seek help and advice at school from your son's class or form teacher. The most positive response is often a whole-class or even whole-school awareness-raising lesson or assembly. It is a bullying issue and, as such, the school should have a position on it – ask them what their policy is. Are they aware of the extent of the issue in school? How are they dealing with it? Do they, for example, take issue with name-calling that is not just racist, sexist or homophobic, but which also seeks to hurt someone just because they work hard? My considered opinion (and you might like to share this with your boy's school) is that we can turn these peer leaders around. They have natural leadership qualities, which is why they command so much power. I believe that if we fine-tune those leadership qualities in a positive way, we can actually turn them into a force for good – give these boys positions of responsibility, so that instead of dragging other lads down into the depths of a mire, they drag them up to the peak of a mountain.

Barrier 9: The laddish culture

The so-called 'laddish culture' is one of the commonest themes of the media in the discussion as to why boys underachieve in schools. Clearly parents on their own cannot hope to eradicate it. But we must try our hardest if we wish our boys to turn into decent young men.

The mildest forms of laddish behaviour in school often come about as a result of boys seeking to avoid the appearance of working so that they can fit in with the rest of 'the lads'. While high-achieving girls in school tend to maintain a positive attitude to their learning all the way through school, we have many boys who are high achievers who often display behaviours of low achievers. Why? So that they can get a licence from the peer police. At the other extreme, laddish behaviour can be used to mask their fear of failure. For those who are lacking in confidence in their ability, being disruptive means that everyone will regard their bad behaviour as the reason for poor achievement. Having a negative attitude to work in a way protects them from failure, as in their minds it often feels better to be seen to be completely uninterested in winning, rather than taking part and losing. Disruptive, laddish, behaviour blurs the relationship between behaviour and achievement and it can also increase popularity. At its worst laddish behaviour can be brutish, sexist and violent.

There is one category of boy in school that tends to succeed and not fall foul of the peer police – the kind who is academically bright and is also good at sport. Why? Because he is clearly 'one of the lads' and therefore he can get away with working. While we can't wave a wand and make all our sons brilliant sportsmen, we can help them to develop the strength of character to resist the worst aspects of laddishness.

We need to:

- Honour our sons' tender feelings – and never hear ourselves saying 'Come on, pull yourself together – you're a boy!'
- Teach them to respect women.
- Encourage their engagement with the arts.
- Show them what a decent man is, how he behaves, talks and treats others.
- Help smash gender stereotypes.
- Ban the phrase 'Boys will be boys'.
- Campaign against T-shirts that say 'I'm a little tearaway'.

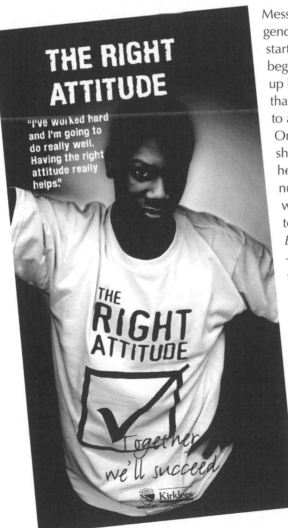

Messages about what is gender-approved behaviour start very young. It often begins around the dressing-up box – 'You can't wear that', one little boy says to another, 'You're a girl!' One parent told me how she remembered that after her son's first week in nursery she suggested they watched a video together to celebrate. She suggested *Beauty and the Beast* – his favourite. 'No!' he snapped. She tried again, several more times. Much to her surprise he resisted over and over again, and in the end was quite vehement, 'No, it's for girls!' He'd only been at nursery for a week. She finished the story by saying that as her son, at the age of 18, left the house for university, the last thing he said to her was, 'Don't throw my Disneys away Mum, will you?'

We need as parents to use every opportunity we can to smash the stereotypes of what it means to be a boy. When boys are very young, quality picture books are useful in helping to break down some of the gender stereotyping and promoting a more caring masculinity. The following are some examples:

- *My Brother Sammy* – Becky Edwards and David Armitage: Sammy is not like other brothers – he doesn't play the same games or go to the same school – because Sammy is autistic. But Sammy does not need special love, for he is like any other brother and needs understanding, patience and acceptance.
  The Lost Thing – Shaun Tan: A very unusual story about a boy who cares for a 'Lost Thing'!
  Man's Work – Child's Play: A board book that challenges stereotypical roles in the home.
  Prince Cinders – Babette Cole: Poor Prince Cinders has a miserable life, looking after his three ugly, hairy brothers! A useful book for exploring gender stereotypes.
  Jump! – Michael Magorian: Every Saturday Steven watches his sister at her ballet class and he longs to join in. But his mother says that real boys don't dance!
  Dad and Me – Jan Ormerod: This book contains four simple, beautifully observed studies of the special relationship between a father and a young child.
  No More Kissing! – Emma Chichester Clark: Momo doesn't approve of kissing. He especially doesn't like being kissed. So he sets out on a campaign to stop it. But then his baby brother comes along …
  The Grandad Tree – Trish Cooke: Leigh and Vin used to play with grandad under the apple tree in their garden. Now grandad has gone, but the tree, like the children's love for him, lives on forever.
  Way Home – Libby Hathorn: This is a dangerous inner city at night and we travel with Shane as he takes home a stray kitten, running terrified from a gang, leaping through screaming traffic, escaping a fierce dog and finally arriving home.

As he becomes older, in addition to the talk that all parents delight in delivering, why not consider a series of other talks too? The following, I find, can be very useful topics for discussion with boys:

- What kinds of behaviours are expected – by other boys – just because you're a boy? Do you ever find yourself having to behave in ways that you would rather not?

- 'Is he man enough?' 'This will make a man of you?' What other phrases do you hear like this and what impact do they have on you?

- What is a hero? Does a hero have to be tough? Can you name people who are heroic, but who are never involved in physical challenges of any sort?

- What is a real man? What do people mean when they say 'Real men don't …'?

- What makes a positive male role model?

- Can you be one some day? (The correct answer is yes!)

Barrier 10: Emotional intelligence issues

Teachers are currently working hard on delivering work on emotional intelligence in schools. It has only recently formally started in primary and far more recently in secondary schools through a package of materials entitled SEALs. Put simply, emotional intelligence is what makes up most of what we are as people. It is said that 80 per cent of a human being consists of emotional intelligence, while 20 per cent is the intelligence we are concerned with measuring in schools via testing. That element of our being that represents four-fifths of what we are is a product of the lessons we learn in life, rather than what we learn in school, and clearly it is of the greatest importance. It is described by psychologist Daniel Goleman as being made up of the following characteristics: Self-Motivation, Empathy, Reflection, Impulse Control, Optimism, Understanding Relationships and Self-Awareness. It's called the SERIOUS model for short. And serious it is as far we are concerned, if we are to bring up decent, caring young men who are also capable of learning effectively.

Self-motivation   We don't help develop self-motivation when we do everything for him. Instead we are encouraging the development of learned helplessness. Neither do we help when we encourage unrealistic expectations, since focusing on the top of the mountain often means he gives up because it always seems so far away. On the other hand, encouraging every independent thought and action and every positive move he makes in the direction of fulfilling his potential while gently rolling the carpet out a little at a time will help. Getting healthy, being active and having enough sleep will help too of course.

Empathy   There is a lot of research, particularly by psychologist Simon Baron Cohen, that makes it very clear that girls and women are, on the whole, better than boys and men. In other words, the female of the species is better able to read emotions in other people's faces as well as to express and discuss emotions. We can encourage empathy from a very early age, through more discussion of emotions with our boys, when sharing stories and talking about friends and family. One powerful way in which we can develop empathy in our sons is to respond more readily to their feelings rather than their behaviour. If your son is angry or disappointed at something that happened at school, it is best to show understanding and respect for those feelings – that way he may just share it with you. In other words, a sympathetic ear rather than questioning what he had 'done wrong this time' or why the teacher had 'had a go at him'.

Reflection   The importance of slowing boys down, encouraging them to take time out and reflect on their experiences and their learning is one of the most important things we can do for our boys.

Impulse control   This is one element that we have to begin to nurture from the very beginning, as evidenced in a famous piece of research in America from the 1960s. A group of 4- and 5-year-old boys were each given a marshmallow on a plate and told that they could either eat it there and then or they could wait until the researcher returned from an errand, at which point they could have two. Some, as you would expect, immediately gobbled down the marshmallows, while others, controlling those impulses, resisted and were duly rewarded. When the researchers returned to visit the boys as adolescents, what they discovered was that the 'marshmallow gobblers' had mostly become socially less successful, stubborn, indecisive and sharp-tempered! In the home, we are teaching impulse control when we are teaching basic table manners, taking turns when playing games and so on.

Optimism   Is his glass half-empty or half-full? For so many boys, when they have made a mistake, they feel that they are a failure. In school, for example, if they get below 7/10, or if the grade is submarine level – below 'C' – and there is no comment from the teacher either written or spoken, then often they will just register failure. What boys need at school and at home are very specific comments about what they are doing right and very specific advice about how they can avoid going wrong in the future if they are to avoid becoming demoralized. And they need lots of praise and encouragement! You might remind him – as mentioned elsewhere – it is only really in education that mistakes are taken as an indication of failure (and boys tend to be the most pessimistic!). In industry and business a mistake is a real opportunity to learn, move on and develop new ideas.

Understanding relationships   Never are we more directly passing on messages to our children than when we show them how relationships should be. In this area we are leading by example every day. We are their main teachers when it comes to showing them how to settle unrests between people who care for each other, and how to talk to members of the opposite sex and show respect towards women. The list is endless. Good role-modelling is priceless.

Self-awareness   The key to developing self-awareness is to help someone recognize and give labels to the emotions they are feeling. Because girls develop facility with language more quickly than boys, this leads them to be more experienced at articulating their feelings and more skilled than boys at using words to explore emotions. For some boys who are unable to articulate their feelings, they can sometimes replace them with emotional reactions such as physical fights. Research tells us also that daughters are six times more likely to use the word 'love', twice as likely to use the word 'sad' but just as likely to use the word 'mad'. What's more, they tell us, when a daughter ask questions about emotions, her mother will give longer explanations and express more sympathy and concern. The answer here is simple: we have to honour our sons' tender feelings and assist them far more in developing their ability to express emotions. As someone famously said, when we give our boys the words to express their emotions, then they will 'unclench their hearts'.

As they grow, boys are learning emotional intelligence in a huge variety of ways, and quite probably more from their family than from anywhere else. It really does start in the home. I often ask teachers to consider the way in which boys are spoken to in comparison with the way in which girls are spoken to in school. Yes, they acknowledge, there is a difference. (Incidentally many boys tell me that teachers talk to boys and girls differently – one summed it up, harshly you might feel, like this: 'Boys get shouted at and girls get talked to!')

Could the same also be true in the home? Do we talk to our sons and daughters differently? And does it matter? One teacher, in his thirties, recently told me, almost tearful at having been reminded of the fact, that all the way through his upbringing his parents had never used his name. 'Come on, son, time for school! All right, son?' I know of no such example of a woman who was just referred to as 'daughter' – do you? Research tells us, and midwives that I have spoken to agree, that from the moment a child is born, if it's a girl the hold is gentler and the voice softer – if it's a boy the hold is firmer and the voice stronger.

As they grow, are there words and phrases that we all too readily use with our boys?

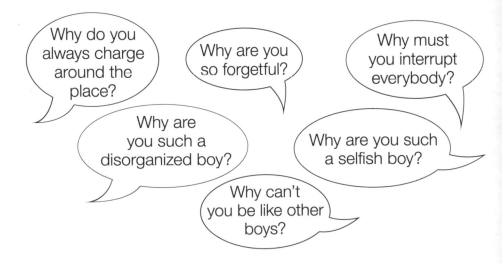

Why can't you be neat and tidy like your sister? (Top tip here: compare and despair!)

Why can't you just be good for once?

Why are you so stupid?

Why do you have to fight with everybody?

Could these be replaced by more positive statements?

What a brilliant performance!

You're a star!

Amazing effort!

I wish I had been as clever as you!

You make me very proud!

Brilliant!

You're a credit to the family!

Why can't all boys be as organized as you?

You deserve to do well!

You're a winner!

You're a pleasure to know.

- Do you tend to be just a little too quick to correct him when he says something that is not in line with your thinking?
- Do you tend to talk in chapters when you're making a point?
- Do you hear yourself using clichés and preaching?
- Do you ever hear yourself projecting him way too far into the future – saying, well if you don't do this now – in 30 years you'll …?
- None of these help!

While we're at it, can we be on the look-out for, and attempt to remove from everyday speech, phrases such as:

- Boys will be boys!
- Well, what do you expect?
- He's only a lad.
- Pull yourself together, you're a boy!
- This'll make a man of you!

Teachers, in their initial training, are taught to balance any negative statement delivered to a child with three positives in order to maintain that child's self-esteem and confidence.

In terms of giving positive encouragement to aid him in his learning, you might find the following useful.

If he says, 'This homework is impossible, I'm not doing it!' and we say 'No it's not, get on with it!' his immediate feeling is that his views are not to be listened to and are therefore unimportant. If we add something such as:

'Algebra's easy, I never had a problem with it!' or 'There's always some excuse – get on with it!', then we are asking for trouble, since his next response, hurt as he is that we aren't listening, is likely to be more dramatic. 'Well, I'm just not doing it – they can stuff it!' On the next occasion he might say nothing at all – he might just not even tell you he has any homework! $\Rightarrow$

If we say 'Don't be stupid, it's easy!', he may believe us – not that it's easy, but that he's stupid! If we tell him he doesn't know what he's talking about, correct him, put him straight on something, then eventually it may well prevent him from ever sharing his feelings or ideas again. If we offer a perfectly logical and reasonable answer to something that's troubling him, it may help him with the problem but it might not make him feel better. However, if instead we listen to an emotional outpouring calmly, and with understanding, his feelings will begin to calm down also and we will get to what is really troubling him. Resisting the temptation to teach him an instant lesson, pull him up short and correct him can be hard, because we can often be far tougher on our own sons than anyone else ever is.

It is our responsibility, as parents, to help guide our children to develop sensitive, empathic communication skills, by *good* example. In his book, *Teenager and Parent* (2003, New York: Three Rivers Press), H. G. Hinot quotes a boy for whom no such opportunity exists.

‘

My father is sensitive to temperature but not temperament. He is totally unaware of emotions and moods. He does not read between the lines, and cannot sense words unsaid. He can talk at length without ever becoming aware that he has lost his audience. He does not see signs of obvious boredom. He never notices that he has lost an argument. He merely thinks he has failed to make his position clear. He talks, but does not communicate. He teaches and pontificates, and runs any conversation into the ground

’

Helping our sons develop emotional intelligence is a massively significant part of what we do as parents, and it starts with the way we are.

Barrier 11: A mismatch between how he is expected to work and his preferred way of working

In schools we refer to three broad learning styles: Visual, Auditory and Kinesthetic. While we can't say with absolute certainty that everyone falls neatly into one or other of these preferred learning styles, most people do show a definite leaning towards one rather than another. You might like to try the questionnaires below. You might also like to try them with your son and hopefully enter into a discussion about how he prefers to learn. Or you might like to try the much simpler 'flat pack' or 'mobile phone' test. It goes something like this: when you, or your son, open up the packaging on either of the above, what do you tend to do? Read the instructions first? Ask someone to read out the instructions while you start to work out how it's put together or how it works? Tip the whole lot out and start putting it together, or start fiddling around to see how it works? Many, but not all, boys and adult males too, fall into the latter category, that of the Kinesthetic learner.

This can lead to some frustrations in school, of course, for example to the boy who is constantly told to sit down, sit still and stop talking. For him you might as well say stop learning, stop learning, stop learning. Never mind toddlers who show a preference for playing in the sand-pit, we still have boys of 15 and 16 who would love to be learning in a more active way. When I asked one group of Year 11 pupils recently what would improve their lessons, one boy replied, woefully, but in all sincerity, 'I just wish they'd let me get up more!'

The following questionnaire is intended as a rough guide to help identify your preferred learning style. Try it yourself and then ask your son to try it. Differences in findings will make for an interesting discussion.

Learning styles test: Visual

Read each sentence carefully. Think about how each applies to you. Tick the box next to the number that best describes how you feel about each statement.

Key: 1=almost never | 2=sometimes | 3=often | 4=almost always

1. I can remember some things better if I write them down.

    1 ☐ 2 ☐ 3 ☐ 4 ☐

2. I am able to visualize/imagine (see) pictures of what I read or am being told, in my head.

    1 ☐ 2 ☐ 3 ☐ 4 ☐

3. I like to take lots of notes on what I read and what I hear.

    1 ☐ 2 ☐ 3 ☐ 4 ☐

4   It helps me to understand what is being said if I look at the person who is speaking.

    1 ☐ 2 ☐ 3 ☐ 4 ☐

5. It becomes hard for me to understand if I don't look at the person who is speaking.

    1 ☐ 2 ☐ 3 ☐ 4 ☐

6. It is easier for me to get work done in a quiet place.

    1 ☐ 2 ☐ 3 ☐ 4 ☐

7. It is easy for me to understand maps, charts and graphics.

    1 ☐ 2 ☐ 3 ☐ 4 ☐

8. When I am concentrating on reading/writing, the radio/TV distracts me.

    1 ☐ 2 ☐ 3 ☐ 4 ☐

9. When I try to remember something, I can see the page in my mind.

    1 ☐ 2 ☐ 3 ☐ 4 ☐

10. I cannot remember a joke long enough to tell it later.

    1 ☐ 2 ☐ 3 ☐ 4 ☐

11. When I am trying to remember something new – a telephone number for example – it helps me to form a picture of it in my head.

    1 ☐ 2 ☐ 3 ☐ 4 ☐

12. When I get a great idea, I must write it down straight away or I'll forget it.

    1 ☐ 2 ☐ 3 ☐ 4 ☐

☐ Total

Learning styles test: Auditory

Read each sentence carefully. Think about how each applies to you. Tick the box next to the number that best describes how you feel about each statement.

Key: 1=almost never | 2=sometimes | 3=often | 4=almost always

1. When reading, I listen to the words in my head, or I read aloud.

    1 ☐   2 ☐   3 ☐   4 ☐

2. I need the chance to discuss things so that I can understand better.

    1 ☐   2 ☐   3 ☐   4 ☐

3. I prefer it if someone tells me how to do something rather than having to read the directions myself.

    1 ☐   2 ☐   3 ☐   4 ☐

4   I prefer hearing instructions rather than reading them.

    1 ☐   2 ☐   3 ☐   4 ☐

5. I can easily follow what is being said without having to look at the speaker.

    1 ☐   2 ☐   3 ☐   4 ☐

6. I remember what people say better than what they look like.

    1 ☐   2 ☐   3 ☐   4 ☐

7. I remember things better if I study aloud with a partner.

    1 ☐   2 ☐   3 ☐   4 ☐

8. It's hard for me to picture things in my head.

    1 ☐   2 ☐   3 ☐   4 ☐

9. I find it helpful to talk myself through tasks.

    1 ☐   2 ☐   3 ☐   4 ☐

10. When learning something new, I prefer to listen to information on it, then do it, rather than read how to do it.

    1 ☐   2 ☐   3 ☐   4 ☐

11. I like to complete one task before starting another.

    1 ☐   2 ☐   3 ☐   4 ☐

12. For a longer piece of work or revision it is easier for me to tape it rather than write it.

    1 ☐   2 ☐   3 ☐   4 ☐

☐ Total

Learning styles test: Kinesthetic

Read each sentence carefully. Think about how each applies to you. Tick the box next to the number that best describes how you feel about each statement.

Key: 1=almost never | 2=sometimes | 3=often | 4=almost always

1. I don't like to read or listen to directions/instructions, I'd rather just start doing.

   1 ☐   2 ☐   3 ☐   4 ☐

2. I can study better when music is playing.

   1 ☐   2 ☐   3 ☐   4 ☐

3. I need frequent refresher breaks when studying.

   1 ☐   2 ☐   3 ☐   4 ☐

4. I think better when I have freedom to move around. Studying at a desk is very difficult for me.

   1 ☐   2 ☐   3 ☐   4 ☐

5. When I can't think of the right word, I use my hands a lot and call it 'thingy' or a 'whatsit', etc.

   1 ☐   2 ☐   3 ☐   4 ☐

6. When beginning to read an article/book, I like to take a peep at the end of it.

   1 ☐   2 ☐   3 ☐   4 ☐

7. I take notes but never go back and read them.

   1 ☐   2 ☐   3 ☐   4 ☐

8. I may look disorganized but I know where everything is.

   1 ☐   2 ☐   3 ☐   4 ☐

9. I use my fingers to count.

   1 ☐   2 ☐   3 ☐   4 ☐

10. I move my lips when I read to myself.

    1 ☐   2 ☐   3 ☐   4 ☐

11. I daydream.

    1 ☐   2 ☐   3 ☐   4 ☐

12. I would rather create my own project than report on someone else's.

    1 ☐   2 ☐   3 ☐   4 ☐

☐ Total

So what are the implications for parents? Well to begin with, it can create a very useful point of connection. Talking about how we learn can be an altogether more positive experience than the occasional attempts at connecting with our sons' educational experiences we may have made in the past: 'I know son, I hated bloody algebra as well, never saw the point of it myself either.' Discussing how he learns, and particularly finding out how he learns best, will also help to develop an understanding of how we might support him in his learning.

Visual learners:

- Can memorize things by writing them out several times.

- Would rather read than listen.

- Like to see illustrations and diagrams.

- Will say things like 'I see what you mean' or 'That looks right to me.'

- Find untidiness quite offputting.

- Doodle when they are bored.

For visual learners, the following are particularly powerful:

- Brainstorming ideas on paper.

- Using highlighter pens to highlight key points.

- Putting notes on index cards.

- Creating maps, diagrams and charts and putting them on the walls of their bedrooms.

- Creating posters containing key bits of information.

- Using different coloured cards to index information.

Auditory learners:

- Would rather be told something.

- Like discussion and debate.

- Talk about things 'sounding good' or 'sounding right' to them.

- Can remember things by repeating them out loud.

- Can be put off by background noise.

For auditory learners, the following are particularly powerful:

- Participating in discussions/debates about the topic they are trying to learn.

- Making speeches and presentations – to themselves if necessary!

- Using a tape recorder to record their own notes.

- Reading text out loud.

- Creating musical jingles/raps to aid memorization.

- Creating mnemonics to aid memorization.

- Discussing their ideas with a group of friends.

- Dictating to someone while they write down their thoughts

Kinesthetic learners:

- Are very 'hands-on' people. They like to try things out.

- They use lots of hand gestures.

- Will memorize things by repeatedly doing them.

- Often can't sit still.

- Talk about something 'feeling right'.

- Can get distracted by lots of movement around them.

For Kinesthetic learners, the following are particularly powerful:

- Taking frequent study-breaks.

- Moving around to learn new things (e.g. reading while on an exercise bike, or walking).

- Working in a standing position.

- Putting the main points on cards then sorting in different ways.

- Chewing while studying.

- Using bright colours to highlight reading material.

- Listening to music while studying.

- Using the process of look, cover, remember, write.

- Skimming through reading material to get a rough idea of what it is about before settling down to read it in detail.

It is important to say, however, that in education it is not just about teaching to children's strengths all the time, it is also about addressing their weaknesses. For this reason in school he should be being taught in a balanced way, through a range of teaching styles. (You might even ask him what ways of learning he actually enjoys most – they will undoubtedly match up with your findings above.) However, there are key times when it is appropriate for him to focus on methods that particularly suit his preferred learning style: for instance, when he is learning something new which he may be struggling with or when he is preparing for tests or examinations.

Barrier 12: Poor reflection skills

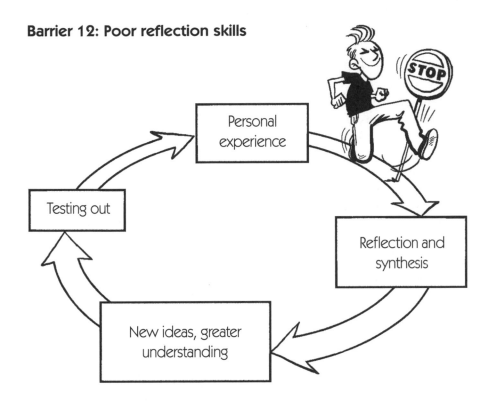

The old saying 'you learn from experience' doesn't quite give the whole picture. We do, in the end, but first of all we have to reflect on those experiences and make sense of them before they can sink in and become new knowledge or understanding. Then we move on to more new experiences and the cycle begins again. For many boys, however, keen just to get on with things and dive into the next experience, the process of reflection is lacking as a result. The amount of learning that can actually take place in these circumstances is somewhat limited. Imagine trying to fill a bath without putting the plug in! In schools, a vital part of the lesson, for boys in particular, is the time when the whole class reviews or reflects, on the learning. It is sometimes called the plenary. At home, the kind of activity that would help develop this vital skill might include the following.

When he's younger:

- Making up stories for him based on his daily life and his own experiences.
- Talking about feelings.
- Encouraging him to talk about what he's doing and what he's learning as he's doing an activity.

When he's older:

- Encouraging him to make a simple memory map of what he's learned in a particular lesson or while doing a particular activity.
- Encouraging him to keep a journal or diary.
- Discussions about what is being learned can be very useful. (Boys in secondary school constantly tell me they love lessons where they just discuss things, but that they rarely have them: 'When we do have a good discussion, we're usually still having it as we leave the classroom!')
- Asking him to write down as many words related to one of today's lesson as he can think of in one minute. (Then ask him what it's all about!)
- Asking him to take the 'hot seat' and answer questions as an expert learner.
- Setting him the task of 'beating the teacher' – with tough questions around the topic being studied.

Generally:

- Discussions about TV programmes or films watched together or what's in the news are useful.
- Getting him to read fiction rather than flick through magazines or factual books will help to develop his reflective skills.

If we are trying to make him a more reflective learner, we are, you might think, in some cases almost talking about a change in personality. Certainly we might be talking about a slight change in lifestyle – for all of you! There is much talk about 'My Space' and the like on computers, no doubt your son has one. But does your family have 'Our Space'? Does someone in the family have someone who will sometimes reach for the off button on the TV or the stereo? Do you ever have a time for silence? Have you ever tried it and then discussed what it felt like? Do you create time just to discuss what's going on in your lives? Is there time to talk about and share each other's interests? Do you look at family photographs together? Unlike the passive watching of screens that transforms us all into a robotic state, these periods can be a real source of nourishment, particularly for the boy who might have spent his entire day in a largely passive state!

Getting out into nature can aid reflection too – gardening, country walks, climbing, fishing. Other reflective hobbies including painting, chess and making music. Tai Chi, Chi Kung, yoga and meditation will all go a long way towards helping him become more reflective, which in turn will make him a more effective learner.

Barrier 13: Low self-esteem and limiting self-beliefs

As a starting-point, consider how much *you* can help raise your son's self-esteem just through normal day-to-day communication. Did you know that when we communicate, only a tiny percentage 'around 7 per cent of the communication', is to do with the words you use. Some 38 per cent is in our tone of voice and the remaining 55 per cent is in our eye-contact, body-language and so on.

> Eighty per cent of your son's self-esteem is in *your* face – in the warm smiles of encouragement, in the eye-contact that communicates appreciation and the gentle nods that indicate understanding.

Self-esteem is a complex area. We often glibly say that someone has got low self-esteem as if it was something like a broken toe that can be fixed. A useful definition by author and educational consultant Bettie B. Youngs divides self-esteem into six component parts and our self-esteem can be pretty low if any or indeed all of the following is missing or in short supply:

- *Physical safety* – freedom from physical harm
- *Emotional security* – the absence of intimidation and fears
- *Identity* – the 'Who am I?' question
- *Affiliation* – a sense of belonging
- *Competence* – a sense of feeling capable
- *Mission* – the feeling that one's life has meaning and direction.

Young, Bettie B. (1986) *Stress Management Guide for Young People* (Austin, TX: Jalmar Press)

Physical safety and **emotional security**   These we supply free of charge in the home in huge doses. That's what parents do. But low self-esteem issues will occur if physical safety and emotional security are in doubt elsewhere – in school for example. That's why, if we suspect, even in the slightest, that he is being bullied or intimidated, then we need to be in touch with school immediately. No question.

Identity   The role models that we as parents present are of course vital, as is the amount of space and freedom we allow him to develop and grow into his own identity. In addition, the more independent we allow him to become, the clearer his sense of who he is will become.

Affiliation   A sense of belonging within the family again goes as read, but to whom is he affiliated outside the home? Our choice of peers is probably the most important choice we make in our lives, and most of us tend to choose 'lower'. (My Great-Auntie Gertrude told me when I was 14, 'Always stick with people who know more than you do' – and it works for me!) But we know too that while girls (and women) thrive more on being part of a whole cooperative and supportive web of networks and relationships, boys often are very different. Forcing him to 'affiliate' in directions we feel appropriate, may not be the best for him.

‘
My dad used to take me to play football for the under 8s, every Sunday morning. He was reliving his own footballing glory days vicariously. I wasn't very good. I was the permanent reserve, standing there in the hail and the snow every week and my self-esteem and confidence was just draining away into the ground on a regular basis.   *Ben, 22*
’

In the case of out-of-school activities, it is crucial that we encourage and support him in areas in which he will not only achieve but also succeed.

Competence   In terms of developing in our sons a sense of feeling capable, we have a major role to play. We must always extend our focus beyond simply how he is doing at school and praise all achievements, not just academic ones. He will thrive and go from strength to strength if he can exhibit his competence in cooking a meal for the whole family, decorating his own room, cultivating an area of the garden, cataloguing the family's digital photographs. But above all, *our* voices – telling him just how capable he is in so many ways must always be louder than those little voices in his head that keep twittering 'I can't do this' or 'I'm hopeless at that'. We need to be forever looking to catch him doing something well.

Mission To give him the feeling that his life has meaning and direction takes time and effort. Even doing it for ourselves isn't always easy. But we are here sometimes to tilt the rudder gently in one direction or another or sometimes to provide a gentle breeze that will help him shift course. Easier said than done? Absolutely. But anxiety is contagious – we know that. We also know from experience that directives, orders, commands delivered in an ill-tempered way can send things way off course. We know, yet sometimes find ourselves continuing to do it regardless. But, as they say, if we keep doing what we've always done, then we'll always get what we've always got! If we recognize that we want to develop in our sons an ability patient, positive and persistent, then what we need to be is exactly the same.

In an assembly of over a hundred 14-year-old boys, I asked how many of them, when they left school, wanted a decent job, somewhere nice to live, a reasonable car and nice holidays – every single hand went up (even the teachers!). Then I asked how many of them thought that was likely to happen. Fourteen hands went up. I've tried it several times since, with the same results, and every time the phrases 'Shooting yourself in the foot' or 'Beating yourself at the first hurdle' spring to mind. Experts tell me that the 'internal auditory' (that little voice inside your head) is louder inside a boy's head than it is inside a girl's! How do they work these things out!? In a sense, it doesn't matter if this is true or not – everyone knows that if you have a little voice inside your head telling you that you can't do something, then the chances are you won't be able to do it. And if you do have that little voice, the last thing you need is for it to have a chorus of backing singers!

I'm allus being told I'll amount to nothing.

A lot of teachers tar us all with the same brush.

One thing my mam always says is 'you're gonna grow up to be your father if you carry on'. He's dead smart – got all As and Bs –but he works in a restaurant.

Limiting self-beliefs and low self-esteem are significant barriers to boys' achievement. Sometimes just their physiology, slumped shoulders, bowed head, can be an absolute giveaway. Try this little experiment:

- Ask a member of the family to stand and raise their arm out in front of them, parallel with their shoulders, and with their palm turned down and flat.

- Ask them to repeat their name out loud in a clear strong voice, over and over again.

- After a few minutes, while they are concentrating, use both of your hands to apply pressure and try to push their arm down, noting how much pressure is required to do so. (Usually quite a lot!)

- Repeat the exercise, this time getting them to repeat a phrase that describes something they can't do, such as 'I can't dance the tango.' But this time in a glum, dispirited way. Wait until they are thoroughly glum about it, then apply pressure again. The difference will be quite amazing.

Does your son ever come out with any limiting self-beliefs, such as:

- 'It's too hard for me.'
- 'I've never had a good mark in maths.'
- 'I'm a terrible singer.'
- 'I tried it before and I couldn't do it.'
- 'I'm never going to be any good at English.'
- 'I'll never understand physics.'
- 'My brother was no good at PE and neither am I.'
- 'I can't see the point.'
- 'I've too much to do, I'll never manage that as well.'

Sometimes we can give these limiting self-beliefs a run for their money just by challenging them with questioning, remembering the basic rule – use his language back to him so that you are honouring (not dismissing) what he has to say. In this way you are also literally 'speaking the same language', not putting it in your language in a way that won't compute.

Or we could make the limiting self-beliefs even worse by offering what we might consider to be comfort.

> Don't worry, I was always rubbish at maths too. You can't be good at everything!

So how else might we turn his self-limiting beliefs around? Encourage him to use positive brain power. To begin with, explain that being positive isn't about saying what it is that you *don't* want to do any more – for example, 'I don't want to be lazy and disorganized any more' – it's about what you *do* want – 'I want to be energetic and organized from now on.' The brain cannot compute the words 'don't', 'do not', 'won't'.

If you need proof, what would happen if someone was to say to you, 'Don't think of a pink elephant'? What does the brain immediately do?

If you believe that you can't do something, then your brain is constantly looking out for all the proof it can to support that statement. It's a little like buying a new bright yellow Mini. Previously you never noticed any on the roads, now you can't move for them. We live in the kind of world that we create for ourselves on a daily basis. If we wake up dreading the day ahead, chances are we'll have a pretty dreadful day. In the words of Henry Ford, if you think you can, or if you think you can't, you're probably right!

Question for your son:

Do you think Richard Branson woke up one day and said, 'Well, I'm not sure, but I'm thinking I might buy an aeroplane or two, and maybe start an airline – but I'm not sure I'd be any good at it' ?

The use of positive self-affirmations is well know to people involved in personal development. How about seeing if he'll try one of these?

Constantly saying 'I don't want to fail' about his next maths assessment means that he probably will! Why? Because he is focusing on failure and maths. Whatever you tend to focus on will tend to show up. It's called the law of attraction. Focusing positively can attract positive results. Positive affirmations have been understood for centuries as a very real way of lifting self-confidence, banishing limiting self-beliefs and improving performance.

It is vital, however, to follow a simple set of rules:

- The affirmation must be written in the present tense: 'I am now working brilliantly and I am getting better and better at maths all the time.'
- The affirmation must contain only *what you want* and *not* what you don't want.
- Display the affirmation prominently in your room and refer to it regularly, repeating it to yourself, and print it on a small card to carry around so that you see it regularly. If it helps, think of this as programming your own internal computer with a programme that only plays positively.

The power of the human brain is immense, bigger than we'll ever know, and we have found out more about the workings of the human brain in the last ten years than we have through the rest of human existence! Recently scientists tracked the brain activity of Olympic athletes as they (a) ran a good race and then (b) as they re-ran it in their heads. The patterns that they traced on their equipment were virtually identical. In other words, the brain has difficulty telling the difference between real and imagined experience. The power of visualization is now becoming widely appreciated. In the face of a big test or exam, encourage him to defeat his self-limiting negative beliefs by using the following technique. You might explain that it is a little like programming your own internal computer. (You might try it yourself if you're going for an interview!)

Exam visualization technique

- Generate the feeling of how it will feel to do well in your next test. First of all find a place to be perfectly still and away from any disturbance.

- Close your eyes.

- *Act as if* the day has arrived and you wake up smiling. Feel the muscles in your face stretch into a smile. Put on your favourite music.

- *Act as if* you are sitting down for a lovely breakfast – it's a real treat. Tasty, yes?

- *Act as if* you pick up your bag, walk out of the door. Feel that bounce in your step as your feet hit the pavement.

- *Act as if* you enter the examination room and sit down, upright and eager. Feel the rim of your chair as you lift it and yourself closer to the table.

- *Act as if* you are leafing through the paper, calmly, and with a growing sense of well-being and confidence. Hear yourself saying. 'That's not a problem', 'I know that', 'That one's easy!'

- *Act as if* you calmly and purposefully begin to write. The pen feels comfortable in your hand and the words flow out onto the page.

- *Act as if* you are taking out just a few minutes to breathe deeply and stretch between questions. Feel the difference.

- *Feel the joy* as your last word is committed to paper. Make that final full stop.

- *Feel the joy* as you return home, throw your bag on the bed and congratulate yourself on a job well done. Put on your favourite music.

There is another technique that you may like to try that is adapted from the kind of personal development work that many successful business people, sports people and even MPs are taught. The approach is called Neuro-Linguistic Programming, which connects language and visualization. One of the key messages of NLP is that the energy flows where the focus goes. This exercise will allow him to focus on that feeling of success and then recreate it at will. Have fun with it!

Don't be an extra in your own movie!

- First of all you need to get 'grounded' – stand straight, eyes closed, feet slightly apart.

- Breathe deeply, from the abdomen.

- Imagine a golden thread from the top of your head holding your head and back perfectly straight.

- See in front of you, on the ground, a circle of light – about a metre across, maybe less – it can be any colour you like – any colour that feels right.

- Imagine yourself staring into that circle of light and start to think of a time when you felt confident and in control.

- See that time clearly – how did it feel? Feel the happiness you felt then. Feel the pride, feel the excitement. Were there people around? Can you hear the noise they were making. Did it make you feel warm? Loved? Appreciated? Feel the warmth.

- See the picture clearly as if it were a movie playing in that circle of light on the ground.

- Now – turn up the brightness on the screen – from 5 to 7 – how does it feel now? Now turn up the brightness and the volume from 7 to 10.

- Now, how does it feel?

- Very gently pinch yourself with your thumb and forefinger, somewhere on your other hand – to check that the feeling is real – it is! (This is called anchoring the feeling.)

- Now step into the light.

- Bathe in it – feel the warmth, the joy. Bathe in those positive feelings very gently.

- This circle of light is yours now – it conveniently folds up into any shape you like and fits neatly in your pocket. It can take any shape. Use it when you need it – shine it over a doorway if you need that extra confidence going into any situation. It is your circle of power – it is all yours, because it came from you. (To bring the feeling back, pinch yourself again just like you did the first time – it triggers the physical memory.)

Barrier 14: Lack of positive male role models

What is it like, as a young boy at one of the key turning-points of becoming a man, going to high school? Some of us will vividly remember it as an exciting/terrifying/exhilarating time. We may recall the fear of having your head flushed down the toilet or being the last person picked when it came to choosing football teams. For many boys it is a period of considerable confusion. Having spent as many as eight years in the same group of friends, on a daily basis, knowing exactly where they stand in the scheme of things, suddenly everything is thrown into the air. From a situation where you felt completely at ease with yourself and life, your strengths and foibles well understood by your peers, you now suddenly have to find a new position for yourself as seemingly countless boys from numerous primary schools are all thrown together at the Big School.

As many parents know, quite a lot can change at the moment of transition, not least a shift in interests. As mentioned elsewhere, the peer police can often make it quite a tough call for boys to maintain an interest in things, such as music and the arts, that are sometimes perceived to be things that real lads don't do. Seeing this as a major concern (what right does a small group of boys have to decide what other boys can do?), I have helped to organize a series of Big Arts Days at one high school in West Yorkshire, where all 300 of the new intake (big school) were hosted by the current

Year 7, and the whole day was spent in groups learning African drums together, doing street dance, learning circus skills, making a newspaper and so on.

One activity that we used every year was to get every youngster to draw a self-portrait on the computer. Of the 450 or so self-portraits produced by the girls, the two below are absolutely typical. Each is beautifully drawn and beautifully symmetrical. Almost every girl portrayed herself as blonde, even though they weren't – can anyone explain that to me?

As for the boys' portraits – below is a completely random sample. Fabulously creative you might say, highly imaginative! But let's look at the influences here – computer and video games, super-heroes and action movies, science fiction and fantasy. The images were almost always full of violent imagery including bullet-holes, skulls, weapons and so on. It begs the big question, where are those positive influences, those role models planted firmly in *reality* that boys so desperately need?

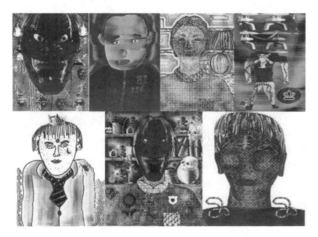

The fact is that many boys do not associate with, or see on a regular basis, any significant older males at all. There are many who never have a male teacher in primary school, for example, or do not experience any male coaching in sport outside of school. Fewer and fewer boys are involved today in groups such as the Scouts or the Boys' Brigade. For these boys, trying to formulate a view of how you should be, they rely upon what they see in the media and in their favoured sport (and some sports provide significantly less positive male role models than others, as we know) to base their version of 'maleness' upon.

For boys, therefore, the importance of the example that older males in the immediate and extended family represent cannot be overestimated. The impact is twofold. In the first area of influence, how older males present themselves can have a huge impact on a boy's development. If we want to turn out decent young men, then we have to show them what a decent man looks like, how he behaves and how he contributes positively to society. The second area of influence is in the area of support and guidance that older males can offer in a boy's education. Yet in many homes some convincing may sometimes be necessary. A headteacher in a high school commented: 'One thing happens time and time again when I phone the homes of children in the school. If it's the father or the male carer in the house, once I have said who I am and explained "I'm just calling to discuss your child", there's usually a brief silence. Then, eventually, the man will say "I'll go get her" and the mother is beckoned to the phone.'

It is not the fault of fathers or male carers, many are simply following the blueprint laid down by their own fathers. But it is time now, in our society, to change the blueprint.

We've always suspected it to be the case, but now there is growing evidence (for example, in the work of psychologist Daniel Goldman) that the involvement of fathers in education can have a significant impact, resulting in:

- better exam results
- better school attendance and behaviour
- less criminality
- higher quality of later relationships
- better mental health.

Importantly, these effects are seen whether or not the children live with the father, and regardless of the level of involvement of the mother.

Fathers and male carers (and grandfathers and older brothers) need to take an active role in boys' education by:

- reading to them
- discussing their day at school
- discussing news of the day
- helping with homework
- working together on a project or on the computer
- offering help in school.

Fathers in the UK now have more time available to spend with their children than any fathers in Europe, according to a recent study. But there are also many more fathers and male carers in today's society who are money-rich but time-poor. Boys need your presence more than your presents!

I was appalled a few years ago when a glossy, government-produced *Parent Magazine* (issue 8 to be precise) contained within its 32 pages only one picture of an adult male – and he was dressed in a tracksuit, watching TV with his son. A few years ago a DVD was issued by the government for parents of Key Stage 3 pupils. It contained eight clueless dads and four really switched-on mums. Of course, parental support of boys isn't just about adult males, but it clearly helps, especially when, as we have seen, the absence of positive male role models can be so unhelpful. To this end, I believe that fathers, male carers, grandparents and other male members of a boy's immediate and extended family could and should be more proactive, not only about their own involvement, but also about increasing the involvement of other males too. There is an element of preaching to the converted here, I know (your engagement with the issue is what made you buy this book!), but what about the hard-to-reach parents?

One school I worked with recently tried, very successfully, to enlist them by ensuring that each parent who regularly attended parents' evenings brought along someone who had never previously done so. Many schools have increased the involvement of fathers and male carers in a variety of ways:

- 'It's a Man Thing' project, focusing on reading, writing and helping to encourage fathers to become more active in their children's learning has been run in Derbyshire, Dudley, Hereford, Bradford, Coventry, Newham and Portsmouth.

- Dads and lads dance project in Gateshead.

- Knitting club – grandads and boys – Cumbria.

- The Youth Sports Trust with community-learning charity ContinYou runs a Top Dads project in schools across the country to introduce young fathers to sport-related play, while offering one-to-one and small-group mentoring guidance on positive parenting.

- ContinYou's Active Dads project runs in schools across Britain to help fathers and other male carers engage with their children through a variety of activities, including reading, walking and going on trips to leisure centres or places of local interest.

- In Lancashire, cricket-loving boys and their fathers are loaned cricket kit, books and activity cards, and encouraged to read together as well as play sport.

- Cookery clubs designed to improve communications and cooking skills between dads and their boys.

All over the country there are:

- Lads and male carers' book clubs

- Male carers' and sons' conferences

- Schools 'Adopting a grandad'

- Bring Dad to School Days

- Male carers' groups that meet to discuss parenting issues

- Saturday morning computer clubs for male carers and sons.

Could you, together with other parents, create something similar, or even something startlingly different (www.fathersdirect.com can help).

As we have seen earlier, many boys need and respond positively to a male mentor, at a time in our history when there appear to be less and less significant older males in our boys' lives outside of their families. Throughout the history of society there has always been a need to provide this kind of support, not least since there can often be a time in male relationships when adolescent boys and fathers drift apart.

> When I was a boy of 14, my father was so ignorant, I could hardly stand to have the old man around. But when I got to 21, I was astonished at how much the old man had learned in seven years.   *Mark Twain*

> Every son, at one point or another, defies his father, fights him, departs from him, only to return to him – if he is lucky – closer and more secure than before.
> *Leonard Bernstein*

Male mentors can also provide those much-needed positive male role models, whether they come from school or from within your own family or circle of friends.

Many schools are seeing the power of developing what I call more caring masculinities by using older boys as positive male role models for younger boys. Often I have encouraged older boys in high schools. (You could try to persuade him to work at his local infant school when it comes to work experience – boys usually do brilliantly well at this, away from the prying eyes of the peer police!)

> When we go reading to the little ones in the junior school, we're the positive role models, 'cos the caretaker's the only bloke there! They think we're like gods!
>
> *John, 12*

One primary school I know in the Midlands paired up a young peer leader from Year 6 with a deeply troubled boy in Year 1, on a daily basis, just to help and guide him through. It was the making of both of them.

> Some days it's tough miss and I have to work hard – but it's great when I can calm him down and talk.

Positive male role models, the kinds that our boys desperately need, do take many guises. You might have an interesting discussion with your own son about who are his positive role models and what characteristics he particularly values and admires. You might also ask him if there is anyone for whom he himself might be a positive male role model, if not now, then some time in the future.

Chapter 2

Let's hear it from the boys

What other reasons are there why boys aren't doing as well as girls?

A group of boys in a Yorkshire comprehensive school explained it to me like this:

Girls? They sit there and don't make a noise and they work well with each other. If lads work together, there's always one that tries to take the lead.

And they're not so bothered about working hard and being smart like we worry, 'cos when we do we're called boffs and that. Lasses don't call each other names.

… and they do their homework!

They listen more too, and concentrate in class.

… and they don't show off like we do.

They stay in and do their work, but we've got a lot more important things to do, especially when you get to the high school.

While a group of boys in Staffordshire offered these thoughts:

Lads mess about more

Lads act cool and hard instead of listening.

Lads get street-cred for getting in trouble.

We are too busy trying to impress our mates.

Boys would rather do more physical stuff.

Girls want to grow up faster than us.

So what advice would they give to younger boys?

- Start working hard early.
- Never leave homework to the last minute.
- Push yourself to the limits – this is your main chance.
- Don't listen to what the bullies say.

These groups of boys are not alone; boys know exactly what the issues are and they also know what it is that they need to do about it. Just talking to boys can be a useful start towards addressing the issues. Persuading them to listen to their own wisdom and take their own advice is the second, maybe slightly harder, step.

Homework

Opinions differ!

Homework? I could do without it really – it spoils my weekend.   *Mark, 11*

Homework's OK if it's for a real purpose – like revision, preparation, for a test and that – but if it's just a worksheet that the teacher's just handed you out as you leave and you know you're never gonna see it again ... well I just don't bother with it. *John, 15*

We do enough at school, why should we have to work in our own time? If they haven't got time to teach it us in school, then why should I have to do it at home? *Steve 17*

It's good if it kind of helps it sink in, what you've done during the day, when it tests you on your learning. *Alex, 13*

School's for learning, home's for chilling! *Errol, 14*

Boys eh? Those 'best barometers of good teaching' are particularly tuned into the value (or otherwise) of homework. Homework is a minefield for so many boys who constantly tell me that they've got 'far better things to do' with their time. Often it can be the cause of serious confrontation when it's not completed either on time or to the satisfaction of the teacher. On the other hand, he may have a point if both of you sense that the homework is sometimes irrelevant, inconsequential, inconsistently set or rarely marked. These things can happen from time to time and they may require parental enquiry at school.

What is necessary is to prevent homework creating another minefield at home. The following strategies may help you, and your son.

How parents can help with homework

● *Getting the facts!* Make sure that you understand the school's policy on homework, including recommended amounts according to the year group he's in and the number of evenings allocated to produce it.

- *Establishing a routine* – say immediately after tea and before leisure time. Some flexibility might be required on the nights he has after-school activities – so why not create a wall timetable that allows for these?

- *Preparing the scene* – ensuring an appropriate workspace is available that is comfortable and appropriately lit (don't worry if he doesn't sit at that lovely new desk you bought him – his learning style may mean he needs to wander from place to place – and besides, he may have been sitting down most of the day at school!).

- *Removing distractions* – and if he's providing his own distractions, such as background music, make sure he is the kind of learner who can cope with this – not everyone can!

- *Establishing a system of rewards* – for completed targets can help. But not 'If you do well this year you can have an i-pod at Christmas'! Short-term rewards work best for most boys – short-term aims, short-term targets and short-term gratification.

Revision

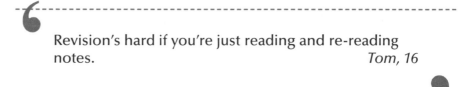

Revision's hard if you're just reading and re-reading notes.   *Tom, 16*

In fact reading and re-reading notes is a pet hate of huge numbers of boys. For teachers, getting boys to read something again, once they have written it, can be virtually impossible.

Certainly, mapping out ideas using simple rules (see planning and preparation) can be a real boon for most boys who do tend to become the kind of learners who not only need to see the big picture but also require a more visually accessible source of information to remember.

Where memory maps are placed on classroom walls to give pupils a big picture of what has been learned and then removed just before tests are administered, teachers note that their pupils are often to be found staring at blank spaces on the wall where the map once was! If neither of you are sold on the idea, just try the following little experiment. Stare at the simple map below for one minute. Now take it away. How much can you recall together? Separately? Did you see pictures/words/colours in your mind's eye? Were your eyes drawn to the place where the map had been opened out in front of you?

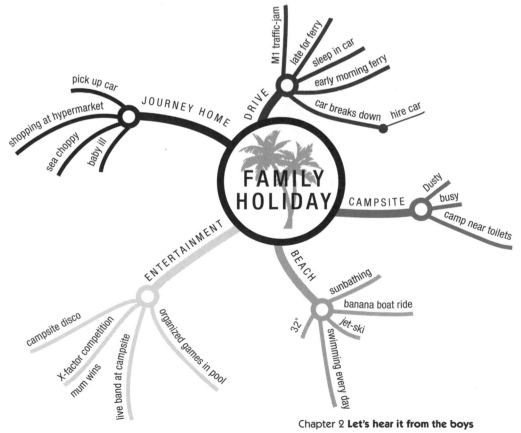

Memory maps can help boys not only to remember things but also to make better and clearer notes that they can access easily and readily. They are also useful in presenting the big picture – reminding them of all the areas they need to cover in their revision. In the context of exam and test preparation, they can also be used to help them get organized (each branch representing a week's study, for example).

Encourage the effective use of interactive online revision sites which

- offer study support
- all work by delivering content in small chunks which are presented and tested
- enable pupils to work in their own time
- provide many opportunities for repeating work
- are non-judgemental
- enable personal target-setting via the individual recording of results.

'Bitesize' (BBC online revision programme) is easy to understand – interesting to use. It breaks the information down – it's already done for you – you don't have to go through an entire book to find out what you need.   *Arshad, 14*

Other online revision programmes to which your school may subscribe, such as Sam Learning, point to impressive research evidence that suggests that a total of eight hours on the programme can make half a grade difference at GCSE (it doesn't sound like a lot, but it can be massively significant). Similar research results are also evident at Key Stage 2 and 3.

More recently, Inquizator, incorporates as the programme's name suggests, a quiz approach; it also has games with state-of-the-art graphics as periodic rewards/'brainbreaks'.

How parents can help around exam time

- *Encourage him to use a wide variety of revision techniques* – staring endlessly at the same set of notes will not help him. The best kind of revision techniques, for boys in particular, are more active, as seen in 'preferred learning styles'. He should spend some time on the computer, reducing notes to index cards – sorting them, creating memory maps/posters/ diagrams/flow-charts – then some time reading notes.

- *Have a quiz* – if he's up for it! The word 'quiz' has a slightly more positive tone to it. (Which would you rather have: a test or a quiz?)

- *Keep an eye on progress* – display exam and revision timetables prominently.

- *Chat to him regularly about his progress* to ensure that he's not leaving everything to the last minute – but don't be overanxious yourself – it's contagious!

- *Encourage him to take breaks* – he needs to take breaks, but ensure the breaks don't take over! If it's on the computer, the break might be ten minutes on a game every hour (real test of will!). Recent revision programmes such as Inquizator, already have games built in as a reward for high scores.

- *Make sure he has some exercise* – even if it's only a stroll outside! Getting more oxygen to the brain will improve his ability to study.

- *Encourage him to talk* – as parents of most boys know, getting him to share any anxieties can be difficult. However, sharing anxieties he might have in the run-up to tests or exams with you, with friends or with a teacher can give a fresh boost to flagging confidence. He may find his mate is worried too and just talking it through will help get it sorted. Similarly, after the event, anxieties need to be talked over to ensure that every exam is a fresh start.

- *Splash out on things to make revision fun and active* – cards, highlighter pens, post-it notes.

- *Make sure he has a decent study environment* – but not too warm – it is said that boys work more effectively in lower temperatures than girls!

- *It doesn't help telling stories about your own school nightmares!*

- *Build in lots of treats in between exams* – and a huge celebration at the end. (You can invite him too!)

Do you know – or more to the point, does your son know – that 66 per cent of mistakes in exams occur because pupils misread questions? I mean, how else would you explain the following, real-life answers to exam questions?!

- What are steroids? They're for keeping carpets still on the stairs.

- What is a seizure? A Roman emperor.

- What does varicose mean? Nearby.

Seriously though, and of course losing so many marks through something so easily avoidable is serious, the brain can play many tricks. Try reading this together, out loud:

The Phaonmneal pweor of the hmuan miund.

Acordnig to rscheerchers at Cmabrigde Uinervisy , it denos't mtater in waht oredr the ltetres in a wrod are, the olny ipnoatmt tihng is taht the frist and lsat leteers are in the rghit pclae.

The rset can be a taotl mses and you can sitll raed it wouthit a porbelm. Tihs is bcuseae the huamn mnid deos not raed ervey lteter by istlef, but the wrod as a wlohe.

It is amazing, the way the brain works. We really are a lot cleverer than we think. On the other hand, and I'm sure this doesn't describe your son, but there are a few boys out there who actually think the opposite – that they are cleverer than they actually are at reading questions, and so steam ahead in completely the wrong direction. Try this little test with him. What does he see here?

Paris in the
the spring

Most people think it says 'Paris in the spring'. If he does too, tell him to remember the phrase 'Paris in the the spring' every time he sits down for a test or exam!

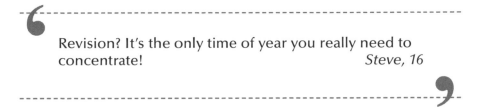

> Revision? It's the only time of year you really need to concentrate!
> *Steve, 16*

If this is the case, how can we help work stick all year round? Well to begin with, talking about his learning throughout the course of a year will go some way towards it. But getting him, from time to time, to teach you what it is that he is learning, as we can see, can really help.

Research suggests that:

- If we are just lectured at, we remember about 6 per cent of the information.

- If we just read about it, we remember about 10 per cent.

- If we get the opportunity to discuss what we're learning, that shoots up to 50 per cent.

- But if we have the opportunity to teach it to someone else, then we will remember 90 per cent of it!

This is a postcard which I designed for Derbyshire Local Authority to send out just prior to GCSEs

Some last minute expert exam tips for students:

- The best kinds of revision techniques are **active**. Use the internet, index cards, memory maps, diagrams and flow charts.
- You **REALLY** know something when you can explain it to someone else.
- Display a revision plan and exam timetable clearly - keep an eye on the **BIG PICTURE.**
- The night before an exam have a good night's **sleep.**
- If you don't **have breakfast**, then by 10.30am your brain will slow right down.
- Drinking **water** keeps your brain sharp and reduces stress.
- **BE POSITIVE** – avoid people who moan and complain.
- **BELIEVE IN YOURSELF** – if you think you can achieve then you're probably right.
- If you start to get wound up in an exam **breathe** in through your nose, counting to three, hold your breath to the count of three, breathe out to the count of three. Repeat three times.
- **TWO THIRDS** of marks lost in exams are because we misread questions so read them **carefully!**
- **Highlight keywords** in questions to make sure you cover everything.
- Show them what you know – **GO FOR IT!**
- **Check** through your work at the end – it's a great way to pick up **EXTRA MARKS.**
- **CONGRATULATIONS** – if you do all the above then you will do really well.

Coursework

> Coursework? I hate it. I just leave it till the last minute. I much prefer tests and exams 'cos you can just swot up on them the night before. *Steve, 15*

> It can put you off a subject! *Shaun, 16*

Coursework has been the downfall of many boys since its introduction in the 1980s. It is currently being phased out in some subjects, but not all. Exams tend to suit boys' risk-taking behaviour, but above all they are fairly instant and soon over with. For many boys, coursework seems just to drag on and on. Many will simply leave it until the last minute either to avoid the protracted agony or because they think 'It'll be right.' (I have come across a lot of boys who think that everything will come out fine in the end without expending too much effort!) As noted previously, short-term targets suit most boys' learning styles and when it comes to getting organized with coursework, I use the term 'boy-friendly chunks'.

It is absolutely vital, however, that boys keep up to date with their coursework – a boy I spoke to recently had been set coursework in September that was due in January, every time the teacher asked to see how it was progressing, he had a different excuse. By Christmas he still hadn't started and therefore hadn't had the benefit of his teacher's support and encouragement (he had though been in detention several times due to his inability to deliver). By this time he was actually too frightened to say anything, because of the consequences. Fortunately for him, he had a good relationship with one of the school's learning mentors. She took him in hand and guided him through a very disciplined approach to his work using a memory map to show the big picture and chunking the work for him in manageable pieces. He got a 'B', but he was lucky.

Helping with coursework

- Find out all of his coursework deadlines.

- Try to find out what is the school's realistic expectation in terms of time spent on each subject's coursework.

- Get him to prepare a timetable containing all the deadlines.

- Agree a regular (supportive) periodic check on progress.

- When estimated grades are provided by the school (usually at least a few months prior to coursework completion), discuss any need to reprioritize.

- Encourage him to share any feedback he's getting for ongoing coursework.

- If things are going wrong, enquire about the possibility of a mentor within school (you may even consider a recent successful school-leaver known to the family).

- Enquire about the range of other support in school, such as catch-up classes.

- Celebrate successes, however small.

- Encourage him to share any worries or concerns with you, his friends, his teachers.

You might also share these, rather more positive, views on coursework from a small group of boys whom I spoke to recently:

It's easy marks!

It's OK, because you can work at your own pace.

It's fine so long as you get it done while it's still in your mind.

Aspirations

> Aspirations? Yeah, I've heard about them, they're a
> tablet you take.   *Josh, 12*

If only! Teachers and parents alike often complain that boys fail to have any aspirations and that this clearly has an impact on the amount of effort they expend on their school studies. Although there is clearly nothing wrong with following in a member of the family's footsteps, by their own admission, this will sometimes impact on their dedication to their studies.

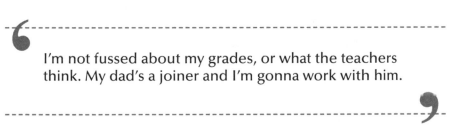

> I'm not fussed about my grades, or what the teachers
> think. My dad's a joiner and I'm gonna work with him.

Unrealistic aspirations can have an equally significant impact on a boy's application to studies. I spend quite a lot of time pointing out to dozens of aspiring England footballers in each school I visit that 'Each year each large town or city in the UK produces just one premiership footballer. Dream of it, go for it, by all means, but what's going to be your plan B?' Boys, unlike most girls, have got a natural tendency to work hardest in subjects that seem to have most relevance for them in real life. In this sense, having a very precise view of what they want to be and what they perceive as relevant to that particular ambition can limit their involvement to a small number of subjects. The challenge, for both schools and parents, is to make clear to boys the links between various elements of learning and 'real life'. This is not always easy. An excellent resource of guidance on this topic can be found at www.connexions-direct.com. By accessing this national website and tapping in subjects of interest, the site will suggest the sorts of jobs that match the subject.

However, there is little doubt that having no goals or targets whatsoever can be demotivating for him and troubling for us as parents. The truth is a lot of boys do have difficulty thinking long-term, in fact getting some to think beyond tea time can feel like a huge challenge sometimes. Many boys need short-term goals and short-term targets. A simple exercise that I have used countless times with boys to help them to roll the carpet out a little bit at a time goes as follows:

Setting short-term targets

Prepare a grid as show below. Decide on a statement, such as 'This is how organized I am' and get him to consider it carefully and honestly, then write that statement in the appropriate column – with 10 = fantastically well organized and 0 as totally disorganized. Ask him then to write down in all the space between the statement and zero, all the reasons why it is not zero (everything he writes will be positive and affirming, therefore). Once this is completed, you then ask him to think about how he might improve his current situation – not to 10 but to the next number (6 if it was 5 and so on). Sometime in the future you might agree to return to the exercise and check for movement towards a particular goal or target, and then set another short-term target.

0	1	2	3	4	5	6	7	8	9	10
These are the reasons why it's not 0					*This is how organized I am*	*This is what I need to do to improve a bit*				

You could use any statement for this exercise, such as:

- This is how caring I am as a person.
  These are the reasons why it's not zero.
  To be a little more caring, I could …

- This is how well I behave at school.
  These are the reasons why it's not zero.
  To improve my behaviour a bit I need to …

- This is how well I'm doing in [choose a subject].
  These are the reasons why it's not on zero.
  For them to think a little more highly of me I need to …

Mentoring, whether carried out by a teacher or learning mentor in school, or by a successful older male perhaps known to the family, can undoubtedly help to raise aspirations, but boys are very clear about how their mentor should be. According to the 2005 Homerton Report (*Raising Boy's Achievement*, London : HMSO) by Younger and Warrington, a good mentor for boys is someone who:

- Doesn't show irritation, but instead has lots of patience.
- Is willing to listen and be enthusiastic for you.
- Is capable of developing a dialogue with you.
- Can convince you of your ability and what you can achieve.
- Is prepared to accept that you are not perfect but can take a positive view of things not just 'go on and on' at you.
- Is straight-talking, honest and genuine.
- Can give advice and support and real strategies to learn.
- Encourages you to take responsibility for yourself, for your time management and for your revision
- Realizes there is life after school!

Even for those who appear to be unmotivated, disengaged, disillusioned, lacking in spark or ambition, all that is often needed is something quite small that will turn them around.

Chapter 3

Boys can be turned around

Recently I worked with a multi-agency group in Staffordshire including church youth leaders, community police, educational psychologists, social workers, teachers, careers officers, representatives of Sure Start, Relate and Connexions. Everyone there had seen success with boys while working with them, provided one or other of the following had been applied, either on its own or in combination with any of the others.

In support of the statement 'I have seen boys turn around when …', they wrote:

- When their families are behind them.

- When they are helped to realize that what they think and feel is important and matters.

- When there is a flexible approach to service delivery which actively involves the boys in the planning and creates the right environment for them.

- When they are set small challenges.

- When they are helped to become good oral storytellers before they are asked to be storywriters.

- When they have been given the opportunity to record their thoughts in ways other than writing, such as diagrams, bullet-points, concept maps.

- When they make decisions that feel right because they know their own preferences.

- When they share active experiences.

- When they have been placed in a workplace and experienced positive encouragement and a realization of why they need education.

- When they are given lots of praise.

- When they are given the chance to lead rather than always being told what to do.

- When they are encouraged and allowed to take risks.

- When they can relate the need to succeed at school to their goals and ambitions beyond school (careers education).

- When they are allowed the freedom to be themselves.

- When they are made to feel that they are the expert or role model.

- When they are given the chance to influence/determine activities.

- When their individual needs are met.

Sometimes it is necessary to explain that just because they make mistakes, doesn't mean that they are a failure. I often ask boys if they know why they call the car maintenance product WD40. They don't, and so I explain that it's because they had made 39 previous attempts to create a successful formula. I make the point that in industry and business mistakes are seen not as an indication of failure but rather as an opportunity.

The following are success stories of individual boys from schools across the country.

> Charlie turned around in Year 10 when I encouraged him at least to *try* the problems, and helped him realize that when he found a way that didn't work he was one step closer to finding a way that did work. He began to attempt the problems and moved from a U to a D.

Sometimes just a change of scene, away from peer pressure or an established routine, can make a huge difference. Or a new challenge can be the spur to move someone on, offering a different arena in which success might come after a series of failures or disappointments in other areas.

> I saw Jordan turn around when he did work experience. His low academic ability was not a problem there. His hard work and desire to please allowed him to succeed. When he returned to school he approached everything with a completely new, a refreshing enthusiasm.

> Jason was given responsibility in a catering kitchen on work experience. He thrived, thoroughly enjoyed the experience and was given a part-time job as a result. On leaving school he took up a full-time position with the same employer and underwent training as a chef. He went to France on his first year placement and he is now an executive chef. For someone who for a long time saw himself as a failure, this has been quite some turn-around!

Sometimes just taking on board a new challenge in school can make a significant difference, often creating a huge positive knock-on effect in other areas of school life too.

'

Tim was persuaded by a mate to enter a school talent show with him. They won! Suddenly he realized that he had something that meant that he would gain the respect from his peers. He recorded it as a turning-point in the school-leavers' book.

Andrew was very nearly permanently excluded from school for poor behaviour. He was encouraged to audition for a leading role in a school production of *Grease*. He got it! From that point on he worked harder in all aspects of school life and he left school with many GCSEs, including an 'A' grade in drama. He is now at college studying drama.

I saw Michael turn around when he was working for a purpose – a medal.

Josh began participating in PE more and going to the gym in his own time. He lost a lot of weight and his self-belief has just gone up in leaps and bounds. His attitude has improved beyond belief!

John couldn't really play basketball, but he enjoyed it. He was given safety to play in – not criticized for mistakes. He passed to the wrong team, he missed all baskets, but he got better. What a smile when he eventually scored (in the correct basket!). A high five

for an uncoordinated, untrendy teenager that all celebrated!

-- **,**

It may well be that your son's school, particularly if it is a high school, has its own system of mentoring. This can have a dramatic effect. It would certainly be an appropriate move on your part to seek out mentoring if you feel your son might benefit like the boys below.

Arjad was one of the peer leaders in school, one of the hardest lads in school, but bright. He was a classic underachiever. He was totally against mentoring. I had to force him to come at first and we talked about everything except schoolwork. I sorted out his college placement and he began to see a purpose in his work. Never perfect, but when he left he sent me a lovely Mr Men thank-you card!

Disaffected and difficult, Callum was one of the peer leaders and he was also on drugs. He was mentored and very closely monitored, and given lots and lots of positive praise. Now he is the most successful member of the mentoring group, and much more approachable. He is also on line for a wide spread of Cs and Bs at GCSE, and on the verge of being a positive male role model for younger boys in the school.

Tom improved because he actually believed that someone was listening to what he said and caring about his viewpoint. This led to an improved dialogue which in turn led to an improved attitude. As a result Tom began to approach his learning and behaviour in a far more positive way.

Hassan changed when he suddenly realized that people cared about him and his future. He made a success of school after staring academic failure in the face.

Jamie started to believe that he had the potential to achieve. He spent time after school working hard on coursework and attended revision classes.

Jack has gone from a being verbally aggressive showman to a far more responsive and self-controlled student who exhibits a desire to succeed. He *loves* praise and affirmation and a bit of respect.

It may even be that your son's school is involved with group mentoring or group support, which again can achieve excellent results.

After years of emotional turmoil, Errol came through In Year 11, with the support of peers and staff, life began for him.

Of course the extra attention doesn't **have** to be provided as formal mentoring. A more positive shift in attitudes by everyone around him can often be enough to affect a change.

Sam turned around when he felt that his parents and school were beginning to acknowledge his potential and giving him specific praise, interest and encouragement.

Even the smallest of steps by both parents and schools can be just what is required. Remember, many boys respond far better to short-term goals. When we are encouraging, them it is often helpful to roll the carpet out a little bit at a time!

> Joe progressed through small challenges and achievable expectations.

Sometimes the school might need to take rather more significant steps in order to encourage improvement in achievement. You may need to enquire about the right move for your son.

> I saw Ali turn around when he was moved into the top set for history. Being removed from his immediate peer group allowed him to shed the mindset of having to be cool. He consistently asks searching questions and makes incisive contributions before his more "intelligent" peers. The impact on his self-esteem and performance has been remarkable.

Sometimes they might even be encouraged to ask for the changes themselves.

> Robin was turned around when he was given the chance (that he had been asking for) to sit the Higher rather than Foundation paper.

Sometimes boys can be turned around as the result of what might be deemed a rude awakening.

‘

Liam took his mathematics GCSE early in November and gained a D He saw that many of his friends in the same group got Cs and although he knew that he had not really worked hard enough, he still expected a C like all the others. His sporting achievements had always given him success and his personality had always got him through. He now realizes that he needed to concentrate more in lessons and not just entertain others. He now has every chance to get a C as he has decided to attend early-morning sessions.

Rob improved dramatically when an anonymous survey at the start of Year 11 showed that other students had highlighted him as a constant disruption in class. He realized then that he had been living in a fool's paradise for four years, believing he was popular and entertaining his mates. Although they laughed with him, the reality was that they were irritated by the constant disruptions and concerned about their education. It was the wake-up call he needed.

’

And then sometimes it just seems to happen mysteriously all by itself!

> Charlie's work improved 100 per cent in recent weeks. I asked him why and he replied that he had had "just decided".

So all is not lost!

Without a doubt, parental involvement and support can and does have tremendous impact.

> John started to succeed when we built up a real partnership between school, home and student.

Indeed, in a recent government report it was suggested that parental support can improve marks by as much as 14 per cent. Where do they get their figures from? I would say, from my experience, that the added value that parents give to their child's education is always hugely significant but virtually immeasurable.

Boys can be turned around: final thoughts

- *Don't panic!* Sometimes talent takes time to emerge.

- Walt Disney was sacked by his newspaper editor because he lacked imagination and creative ideas.

- Einstein couldn't speak until he was 4 and couldn't read until he was 7.

- Beethoven's music teacher told him he was hopeless as a composer.

Chapter 4

How schools are responding to the problem

This book has focused primarily on those barriers to boys' achievement which, I feel, parents can usefully contribute towards removing. Below and on the following pages is the full range of barriers to boys' achievement, and some examples of the kinds of things schools are doing that are having a positive impact:

Barrier to boys' learning	Typical examples of work in schools that do help break through the barrier
Lack of independence prior to starting school	Parent information sessions on the importance of developing independence in boys. Many Early Years settings start to contact parents some considerable time before school begins.
Less developed linguistically on entry to school	Parent information sessions on the importance of the development of communication skills pre-school. Organizations such as Sure Start and I Can offer useful support materials.
Being forced to read and write before they are physically or emotionally ready	Most Early Years settings are involved with projects such as 'Write Dance' or other work which focuses first on getting the gross motor skills working before looking at on the fine-motor skills boys need. Lots and lots of fine-motor skills development exercises go on before writing is attempted.

Barrier to boys' learning	Typical examples of work in schools that do help break through the barrier
Playtimes for boys tend to be hyper-physical and boi(boy!)sterous	There is now more structured play in playgrounds, often run by play leaders, and sometimes supported by the pupils themselves in the role of playground buddies. Giving pupils responsibilities for the organization of activities often ensures a calmer atmosphere and boys (girls as well, of course) respond well to responsibility.

Also many schools provide alternatives for those boys who don't always want to be charging around in what can be, for some of them, a quite intimidating atmosphere.

Some enterprising primary schools now include activities such as peer massage to calm children down after boisterous play – it helps take some of the 'macho edge' off and get the youngsters in the right emotional state for learning. Peer massage also helps boys in particular to develop empathy. The power of positive touch is immensely calming and therapeutic. |
Many writing activities in school perceived as irrelevant and unimportant	To engage boys more effectively in writing, many primary schools now focus much more on using discussion and drama-based activities to enable boys to talk through their ideas first. A strong emphasis on writing for a real purpose and a real audience, at any level, does engage more boys – as does a significant reduction in the amount of 'copying out' in lessons.
Boys' difficulties with structuring written work	In primary schools there is an increase in approaches such as 'Big Writing', which is the kind of systematic approach which has boy-appeal. As boys move through school, there is also an increased focus on the use of graphic organizers, mapping and learning mats – all of which help them to structure their writing. The main strategy that teachers will be using is 'modelling' the way it should be by giving specific, detailed examples. Lots of talk is also used as a way of helping boys to structure their ideas before putting pen to paper.
Boys' reluctance to spend time on planning and preparation	The mapping-out of ideas is being used most effectively to speed up and simplify the process. Schools are also beginning to develop research skills earlier and earlier for boys, mindful of their tendency to just 'cut and paste', even at the age of 16.
Reading fiction perceived as a female province	Parent information sessions about the importance of male role models in the house reading and supporting boys' reading are quite common in primary schools.

Barrier to boys' learning	Typical examples of work in schools that do help break through the barrier
Teacher talk/teacher expectations	Teachers are increasingly aware that developing emotional intelligence in children starts with the adults around them. Many schools now, through classroom observation, look at the differing ways in which they talk to boys and girls, and address any negativity as a result.
Emotional intelligence issues	At the time of writing, all primary schools have been involved in the delivery of emotional intelligence materials (called SEALs) and all secondary schools are due to start implementing the work. The work includes a focus on developing impulse control, empathy and self-motivation. These, and many more of the areas covered by SEALs, are particularly significant for boys.
Mismatch of teaching and learning styles to boys' preferred learning styles	There is a far greater awareness of the fact that teachers tend to teach in the way in which they learn best – and the vast majority of teachers are visual learners. As a result, practice has been changing rapidly, and in most schools the full range of teaching styles are used in a balanced way, ensuring that all learners (and we have many boys who prefer to learn in a more active way) are catered for *and* extended in areas of weakness.
Lack of opportunities for reflective work	Schools are often increasing their focus on plenaries (reflective elements of the lesson) and developing as many opportunities to reflect and review as possible. Schools are also becoming increasingly aware of the significance (for boys in particular) of encouraging and developing skills in such diverse areas as reading fiction, yoga, meditation, visualization, etc.
Pupil grouping	In terms of 'setting' pupils, many schools are clear about the negative impact on the self-esteem and motivation of boys who are in bottom sets, and some have reverted with great success to mixed-ability teaching. Schools have experimented with and largely abandoned single-sex classes for certain subjects in mixed comprehensive schools. There has been some limited success but far more instances of boys-only groups becoming more 'laddish' and their attitudes to learning becoming more negative.

Barrier to boys' learning	Typical examples of work in schools that do help break through the barrier
Inappropriate seating arrangements	Many schools have a clear policy on seating, which at least states that teachers decide where pupils sit. Flexibility appears to work best, where boys get the chance to sometimes work with their friends, sometimes with members of the opposite sex, and sometimes with people they would never dream of working with. Where schools have tried seating pupils boy/girl/boy/girl there has been limited success in terms of raising boys' achievement. Some schools have cited improvements in behaviour, but my research shows that by and large girls dislike it and boys tend to rely on girls' help.
Ineffective group work	As schools develop an understanding of how boys work best in groups, more attention is given to making sure that there is a clear goal, that everyone has a particular role, that the activity is time-limited and there is an element of challenge to the work.
Peer pressure (anti-swot culture)	Peer leaders in schools are natural born leaders and, increasingly, schools are becoming aware of the advantages of providing these boys with leadership training that has a *positive* focus. In many cases, boys have been turned around, as we have seen. Some schools are effectively raising awareness of the issue through assemblies, PSHCE, school bullying policies, etc.
Inappropriate reward systems and the lack of a positive achievement culture	The fact that many boys feel that celebrating success is not a cool thing to do is largely due to peer pressure. Where schools are managing to overcome the stultifying grip of the peer police and effectively encouraging enthusiastic celebration of achievement, they have employed a range of strategies. These include: involving the school council in determining what pupils want as rewards and how they would like to be rewarded. Many schools have returned to the old 'house' system – that means that everyone (including the peer police) benefits when rewards are won. 'Praise postcards' sent home enable pupils to celebrate their successes at home – sometimes for the first time!
The laddish culture	Work in schools to promote boys' engagement with the expressive, creative and performing arts is fundamentally important in the battle to develop more caring young men. Engaging them, as many schools do, in some form of peer support clearly also helps.

Barrier to boys' learning	Typical examples of work in schools that do help break through the barrier
The influence of street culture	Actively acknowledging some of the more creative elements of street culture within schools, such as the better examples of street art, music and dance, has engaged some adolescent boys, whereas a refusal to acknowledge its existence would have presented an additional pressure for boys to take to the streets.
Mismatch in assessment and examination methods to boys' preferred ways of working	Most boys much prefer examinations to coursework, as we have seen. Better still, boys would prefer to be examined orally – not having to write anything down. While coursework exists, and remains a significant barrier to boys' achievement, many high schools have devised ways of improving boys' coursework grades. Most effective is the 'chunking' of coursework, which involves setting a series of deadlines for a series of 'chunks' or chapters of coursework.
The lack of positive male role models	In some 'clusters' or 'families' of schools, much imaginative use is being made of older boys operating as positive male role models for the younger ones. They help with sports tuition, assist in developing reading skills, write stories for younger children or help organize drama. Older boys taking part in work experience at their local primary schools provide male role models where sometimes these are non-existent. In some schools, those significant boys I refer to as the peer police are used in a variety of ways to promote positive learning behaviour – in posters, in assemblies, leading activities, in school councils, etc.
Use of drugs	Research has suggested that drugs education has been of limited value. Some schools are now beginning to address the issue more intensively in the light of boys' increasing engagement with drugs generally and with (increasingly more potent) cannabis in particular.
Self-limiting beliefs	Schools are beginning to introduce the kind of work on self-development and self-improvement commonly used for adults.
Lack of engagement with the life of the school	Many schools are aware of the need to engage boys in the life of the school to raise self-esteem and motivation. Projects include peer-mentoring schemes, shared reading schemes (where older boys help younger ones improve their reading), school councils, sports councils.

Barrier to boys' learning	Typical examples of work in schools that do help break through the barrier
Homophobic bullying	Schools are becoming increasingly aware of the need to incorporate homophobic bullying into their bullying policies. However, progress is painfully slow. The statistics presented in 'Stand Up For Us' show that 40 per cent of gay youngsters who have suffered homophobic bullying at school have attempted self-harm, while 20 per cent have attempted suicide. The most recent report from the government suggested that only 6 per cent of schools had such a policy.
Lack of parental understanding of raising boys' achievement issues and their inability to offer appropiate support	Many schools have begun to organize awareness sessions and/or produce information leaflets on the specific subject of raising boys' achievement.
Intervention occurring too late	With the increase in data on our children's development, as we have seen, it is clear that we need to get it right from the start. Early Years units are increasingly aware of the need for this. As a result, there is an increased focus on fine-motor skills development, the significance of active and outdoor play, the importance of parental support, the importance of combating gender stereotypical behaviour and so on.
Teachers' lack of awareness of issues related to gender and achievement	There has been a growing increase in awareness brought about by the number of courses and publications on this specific issue.

Conclusion

And finally ... PASS IT ON!

What can parents do *together* to help raise boys' achievement in school? Well, you could meet together and share your own experiences, your problems and the solutions that have worked for you. Maybe your school would consider hosting such a meeting? As all teachers realize, the people who know what makes their children tick are, first and foremost, the child's parents. While you may have picked up some useful information and some helpful tips, you may also have been sitting there thinking, 'Well actually what works best for me is ...' and 'Well, I can see what he means, but I also tried ...'. This book only scratches the surface of the problem. Every parent has something to offer in this debate. I have run countless parents' evenings and as a result of a few of them we have, together, produced materials to use with all parents, sometimes for a particular school, and in one case for hundreds of schools. The leaflet below was produced by parents at the school where I was working in the 1990s. Parents were given a presentation of the facts (as outlined in the first chapter of this book), and then, working in small groups with a teacher, were encouraged to put together a series of tips for other parents on how they might help their boys at home. (I have also included here additional explanations of the points raised.)

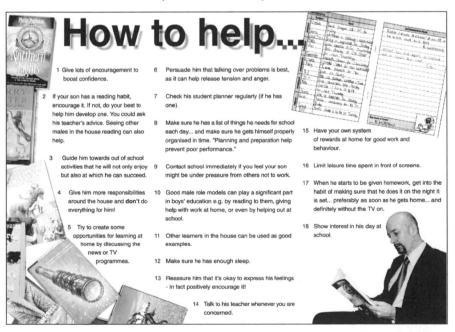

How to help...

1. Give lots of encouragement to boost confidence.

2. If your son has a reading habit, encourage it. If not, do your best to help him develop one. You could ask his teacher's advice. Seeing other males in the house reading can also help.

3. Guide him towards out of school activities that he will not only enjoy but also at which he can succeed.

4. Give him more responsibilities around the house and **don't** do everything for him!

5. Try to create some opportunities for learning at home by discussing the news or TV programmes.

6. Persuade him that talking over problems is best, as it can help release tension and anger.

7. Check his student planner regularly (if he has one).

8. Make sure he has a list of things he needs for school each day... and make sure he gets himself properly organised in time. "Planning and preparation help prevent poor performance."

9. Contact school immediately if you feel your son might be under pressure from others not to work.

10. Good male role models can play a significant part in boys' education e.g. by reading to them, giving help with work at home, or even by helping out at school.

11. Other learners in the house can be used as good examples.

12. Make sure he has enough sleep.

13. Reassure him that it's okay to express his feelings - in fact positively encourage it!

14. Talk to his teacher whenever you are concerned.

15. Have your own system of rewards at home for good work and behaviour.

16. Limit leisure time spent in front of screens.

17. When he starts to be given homework, get into the habit of making sure that he does it on the night it is set... preferably as soon as he gets home... and definitely without the TV on.

18. Show interest in his day at school.

It is, I believe, vital that we spread the word about the barriers to boys' achievement and raise parents' awareness of the issues. I also believe that we need to communicate to all parents the importance of developing boys' independence and why and how we need to develop language skills. Some of the most significant barriers to boys' achievement, such as peer pressure, low self-esteem and limiting self-beliefs, need to be broadly aired and more widely understood. Spreading those messages around about the importance of positive male role models and the huge significance of parental support I now hand over to you. PASS IT ON!